FOLLOW THE OTHER HAND

FOLLOW

THE OTHER

HAND

A Remarkable Fable That Will

Energize Your Business,

Profits, and Life

ANDY COHEN

iUniverse, Inc.
New York   Bloomington

iUniverse books may be ordered through booksellers or by contacting:

iUniverse
1663 Liberty Drive
Bloomington, IN 47403
www.iuniverse.com
1-800-Authors (1-800-288-4677)

ISBN: 978-1-4401-3088-5 (sc)
ISBN: 978-1-4401-3089-2 (ebook)

Printed in the United States of America

iUniverse rev. date:03/16/2009

*Dad, hope there's a bookstore
in Heaven so you can read this.
P.S. Tell U.G. I'm still practicing magic.*

CONTENTS

SECRETS REVEALED

This business book is a fable full of "magical" secrets. Newly revealed strategies on how to think differently, how to increase your sales, and how to generate new ideas. Captivating ways that will provide you with a competitive edge.

Along with these secrets comes some magic. I have included magic lessons that will turn you into a mind reader and a regular Houdini.

Every "business" secret in this book is fun to learn and easy to apply. They will open up new doors of opportunity regardless of whether yours is a business of one or one hundred thousand.

The techniques you'll learn will amaze, entertain, and energize you. By the end of the book you'll be filled with more ideas and innovative solutions than you will know what to do with.

And while the word "secrets" may have intrigued and motivated you to read up to this point, when you finish the book, you'll discover that knowing a secret is just the beginning. What truly brings you success is something that has resided in you since the day you were born.

But we'll save that lesson for the end of the book.

Meanwhile, get ready for a remarkable story that will change the way you think forever. And that's no secret.

I deas are what keeps business alive. Without a constant in-
flux of new ideas, any business will slowly flicker like a
candle in the wind and, eventually, die.

JetBlue had a great idea—let's treat airplane passengers like
human beings again—and they put it into action. As a result,
JetBlue keeps growing, adding more and more routes, producing many thousands of happy customers. Starbucks envisioned
a fifty-cent cup of java as a three-dollar experience; it's now testing the concept of evolving into a music store that also serves
up that java. Starbucks's constant evolution shows us that the
best companies never stop generating new, exciting ideas. GM
realized that the future of the auto industry went beyond fast
and comfortable cars and conceived a great new idea: a com-
munication service called OnStar. First, OnStar increased GM
customers' satisfaction; then, it morphed into something entirely new. OnStar's automotive development process became
the catalyst for the meteoric rise of the satellite-radio industry.

The big difference between today and decades past is the
speed at which ideas must come for businesses to thrive. The

slow nurturing of ideas is a luxury that is now behind us. IBM reminds us that we live in an on-demand world. Dell lets us customize computers that are shipped within twenty-four hours. Lands' End lets us design our own clothes on the Web. Build-a-Bear Workshop allows children to make their own stuffed animals with personalized voice recordings inside. These innovative business ideas went from inspiration to execution in record time.

To survive today, you must be able to come up with more than just great ideas; you also need to be able to produce ideas on demand. To accomplish that task, you have to explore new ways to innovate.

Competition for time, money, and space demands that we think differently to stay ahead. At home, we have to come up with new ways to balance work, family, and friends. At work, we are told to think out of the box and to be creative or risk obsolescence in our careers. Collectively, we struggle with finding creative ways to keep up, to stay competitive, to adapt to new technology, and to succeed.

But as the world demands new ideas, it also resists them. At most companies, true innovative thinking is allowed so long as it's "safe." Thinking outside the box is accepted—if it comes with a guarantee that it works. Executives buy into new ideas only if they have seen the ideas executed somewhere before. Creativity is fine, as long as the new ideas are not so fresh and original that they trigger our fear of the unknown. This reality dictates that you need to reexamine how to present ideas and persuade others to adopt them. Failure to do so is not an option: More than ever before, obsolescence is fatal.

My goal in writing this book is to help you produce new ideas on demand by unlocking your creativity and to give you the tools to put those ideas into action. The process uses the principles of magic as metaphor for thinking differently, generating new ideas, and implementing innovative business solutions.

The use of magic as metaphor may seem implausible. But so, too, were the ideas of charging $3 for a cup of coffee; or charging $120 a month for what used to be free TV; or asking as much as $2.99 for a ring tone on your phone. In fact, at one time, I was a skeptic about the concept of mixing magic with business. I thought that magic was fine as entertainment, but when used as a metaphor with business, people would immediately think of "illusion" and "trickery." This type of response would provide an insurmountable obstacle to the benefits of the message.

A long-standing friend and business associate named Stan Rapp thought differently. Stan is an icon in advertising. He is the cofounder of the world's number-one global direct-marketing agency, Rapp Collins, and bestselling author who predicted the rise of one-to-one marketing. Stan knew of my success in helping companies generate hundreds of thousands of dollars in sales through creativity and new ideas. He knew of the fifty-some industry awards I have received. He also knew of my history with magic; how I began performing when I was six under the influence of my magician great-uncle; my appearances in nightclubs and on national television; and my use of magic to warm up my audiences during lectures on innovations in marketing, sales, and advertising. Stan believed in the idea that the magician's performance has a parallel in the performance of outstanding business leaders. Both have a way of disarming defenses, making people open to new avenues of learning, and leaving the audience with a long-lasting impression. (Who doesn't have a childhood memory of having a coin pulled out of his or her ear?)

Pushed by Stan, I began exploring new ways of using the world of magic to teach business creativity and execution. It took me a year of thinking, researching, and using friends and business peers as "guinea pigs" before I developed the confidence to believe that magic does indeed work as a metaphor.

I quickly found out that the business world agreed. Executives from big global companies like AOL, Nestlé, and L'Oréal embraced the concept that this two-thousand-year-old art of prestidigitation holds secrets, methods, and processes that could help the business world solve problems.

Since my expertise is in marketing, I will draw upon examples from advertising, branding, and sales. Yet my conclusions can be applied to a range of business challenges—from change management to organizational development, to new product development and technological innovations. While the focus is on business, I hope you will also find yourself instinctually applying the lessons to your own personal life.

A quirky magician by the name of George Miles—trade name Merlin—will teach the lessons in this book. Merlin is part me and part personification of all the famous and talented magicians I have met in my life. These include: Al Flosso (the Coney Island Fakir), Tony Slydini (the legendary close-up magic artist), Dunninger (a great mentalist and legend), and the real George Miles (a true vaudevillian magician and, in real life, my great-uncle).

As a twenty-five-year member of the Society of American Magicians, I honor my pledge to uphold the principles of magic. Any secrets revealed are those that either are commonly discussed or pose no threat to the livelihood of magic professionals. You, on the other hand, are under no obligation to share the secrets revealed in this book. You may choose to keep to yourself the business lessons that you will learn in this book as they will assist you in your path to newfound success. But my experience teaches me that, like any great magician, you are going to show off the effect of success with pride.

FOLLOW THE OTHER HAND

HOW I MET MERLIN—MY PREDICAMENT

I, Jonathan West, like to tell people that I am in the oil business. Their eyes light up and I can watch them mentally calculating how much money I am worth. I can almost see them imagining mansions in Texas and meetings with sheiks and princes in the Gulf states.

Then, waiting a beat, I explain that I am in the *olive oil* business. I import olives, olive oil, and related gourmet products. The bubble bursts and I am once again an ordinary, if not boring, guest at a dinner party.

If they had the interest and I had the time, I'd share with them a story that's both wonderful and tragic. It's the story of my great-great-grandfather who came to America penniless, spoke no English, and was taught by a very cruel person that saying "screw you" was how one thanked people in his new country. After many fistfights, my great-great-grandfather figured out what he was saying, plunged into learning English, and began to make a living. You've all heard stories of the immigrants' struggles after arriving in America, and his was no exception. Life was hard, but fortunately over time things began to pay off. The Dutch gene in him made him a natural at trading and selling. He became a middleman, moving buggy whips, pool tables, baby dolls, and olives. Apparently, there was a lot of money in these pitted fruits, and he founded West and Company, the import business I run today and hope to continue running. But things at West and Company are so tough that there's a serious chance I will have to close or sell it.

My business is in trouble. I'm a middleman, you see, and we all know from the success of Michael Dell that, in today's economy, the middleman is dispensable. Technology now allows both customers and companies to buy and sell direct. Our service, at least the way it's currently perceived, is quickly becoming obsolete.

Adding to my woes, many of the local mom-and-pop stores that sell our products are being forced out of business by much larger supermarket chains. These larger shops are merging, and our flow of sales is falling victim to consolidation. These chain stores are in turn being squeezed by the big-box stores like BJ's and Costco, who are being squeezed by the biggest retailer of them all, Wal-Mart. As we go up this chain, prospects get worse and worse for West and Company.

We are losing our long-term relationships on both ends. Our leverage on both sides, suppliers and retailers, has shrunk, along with our profits. The big-box stores can simply dictate our pricing, and, you bet, that's what they do.

I've saved over the years, so if the business went under, my family and I would survive. But like any family businessman, I've been haunted by a peculiar fear that keeps me up at night and worried all through the day. You could sum it all up in one word: "legacy." I couldn't face being responsible for ending three generations of business, firing a hardworking and loyal staff, and starting some type of new career from scratch.

Change had happened and I hadn't adapted fast enough.

The old family formulas of selling were no longer working. E-mails had replaced face-to-face sales calls. Our products were "terrific," but so were everyone else's. You don't get gold stars for terrific anymore: There are just too many products and not enough customers. As revenue slipped, so did the performance of my employees. Morale was as low as sales, and I was beginning to hear "it can't be done," "we don't have enough time," and "we've tried that already" all too often. I needed new ideas. New solutions. I needed to think differently about my business and do it fast.

I needed a different perspective, so I called a buddy of mine, Wilcox, for lunch. We were college chums, and while I studied psychology, he played guitar and skipped classes. After graduation, Wilcox gave guitar lessons for a living—then opened a guitar center—then expanded into a chain and then sold the business for a respectable profit. He then went back to school, got an MBA, and founded a business that recycles tires into rubber flooring for home and industrial use. He was always full of energy and never without an idea. My other motive for the call was an unrealistic belief that his counsel would provide a magic solution to all my problems. And it did, but in a way I never suspected.

While we were waiting for our food I brought Wilcox up to speed and told him I needed new ideas to stimulate sales and keep the business growing. Maybe he sensed my desperation, I don't know, but Wilcox seemed very willing to help. He had a curious little smile, almost as if he was setting me up for one of those practical jokes he loved to do in college. He told me there was good news and bad news. I asked for the good news first.

"Jonathan, the good news is, I know someone who could help. But here's the catch: To have him help you, you have to keep an open mind." That's it? I thought. Maybe it was my frame of mind, but this "bad news" wasn't so terrible.

"This guy helped me when my guitar centers were heading in the wrong direction," Wilcox informed me. "He's a genius. He will challenge the way you think from the moment you meet him. You could say his method is unorthodox but highly effective. He made me think differently about the way I do business. He taught me new ways to get people to buy a product and showed me how to profit from changes in technology. He revealed to me how to identify the essence of what makes me unique."

"So, what's the deal?" I asked. "Is he some megabucks consultant who will only see people who pay him hundreds of thousands?"

Wilcox smiled as he shook his head no.

"His name is George Miles," Wilcox continued. "But he will ask that you call him by his trade name. I'll keep that a mystery for now."

Wilcox gave me George Miles's number and told me to make an appointment.

"What kind of trade?" I asked. "Is he a consultant, past CEO, or a successful business entrepreneur?"

"He's a magician," was the reply, "and he's one of the reasons my new business has grown 28 percent this year."

OK, I thought, a magician. "Is he going to wave his little wand and double our revenue?" I asked.

Wilcox listened and said he understood my skepticism completely. He confessed that, a while back, he faced a similar crisis in keeping his guitar centers from stagnation. One of his entrepreneur friends suggested that he meet with George Miles. He thought the whole thing was a joke when he heard that Miles was a magician. But now he swore by the man.

"I can only tell you that it will change the way you do business forever. Business needs a constant stream of new marketing ideas to grow, and you will learn how to keep generating them. Business needs to help employees get out of the rut of saying, 'It can't be done; it costs too much; I don't have the time to do it.' Business has to learn how to use technology in ways the competition never considered. Business has to constantly relearn the basics of reaching out to customers and motivating their response. Business has to learn to think differently to survive."

I was still skeptical and Wilcox sensed it. "Tell you what," he said, "I believe in George so much that I will send you a check to cover the first visit. If you do not get anything out of it, hand George the check. If you use what he says, you pay. Nevertheless, keep the check. If at any time you feel you haven't gotten your money's worth from one of the lessons, use the check." I later learned that Wilcox, by providing me with choice and control, was applying lesson two, called "Building Trust—Making the Audience Part of the Act."

As I headed back to the office, my spirits lifted. I began to imagine that things were not as bad as I suspected, that I was overreacting, that we just needed a break that would turn the business around. Riding up the elevator, I looked in the mirror and realized I was scared and I didn't know how to share that fear with my team.

You see, my personal history and the history of West and Company were so entwined it was like we were like two peas in a pod. I hadn't intended to go into the family business; when I went to Franklin and Marshall College in Lancaster, Pennsylvania, I had been set on studying psychology, with the plan of going on to graduate school and becoming a clinical psychologist. I loved the field and was fascinated by how and why people behaved. Turns out, I wasn't fascinated by the prospect of spending the next eight years in academia. I took a rain check on getting that degree.

My studies in school trained me to think empirically, which

contrasted with the way I approached cooking (I never followed a recipe) and bike riding in Europe (I created my own routes). My dad perceived that these conflicting ways of thought would make me an ideal candidate for the family business, which required a passion for gourmet foods, a love of travel, and a mind for business. He saw my hesitation in going after a degree and began his campaign to recruit me to sign up to West and Company.

He was right. I've been eating bread drizzled with olive oil since I was two. When I was ten my grandfather taught me the art of testing the quality of a wheel of cheese by using smell and feel, examing the rind, cutting it open, smelling it again, tasting it, taking an iron, and pulling a plug out as a final test. I could name seven different types of mushrooms before I started high school. The business was in my DNA. The family joke was that my blood type was "extra-virgin." Even after I was married.

So my new home became the familiar offices of West and Company, located in six thousand square feet of loft space in New York City's Soho district, one of the most popular retail destinations in Manhattan. It's housed in a five-story building, constructed in 1859, which my grandfather moved into when people still had horse and buggies. My father, along with some associates, purchased the building almost a hundred years after it was built. Walk into our office space and you immediately sense that "heritage" is very important to us. It provides a vision and standard for our family-oriented service. We still have the old three-foot-wide oak floors that gently creak as you walk, an old fireplace that we gather around to do our product tasting on cold winter days, and when you look up, you see the sparkly, tinned ceilings that designers today charge a fortune to replicate.

It's an open space that is roomy enough for my forty employees. You can see from the back of the office to the sixteen-foot windows in the front of the loft. The back half of the office contains our kitchen, storage, bathrooms, freezers, and freight elevator.

Our conference room is in the center of the office. Industrial-type Metro shelves twelve feet high—the kind you see in restaurant kitchens—frame the room on three sides. These shelves are constantly being stocked and restocked with olive oils, cans of olives, tins of crackers, bottles of sauces—items we are testing as well as selling. The top of the conference room table is the refurbished loft door of our space. It's surrounded by eight modern-looking Ikea chairs, two computers used for tracking inventory and videoconferencing with our international suppliers, and a small refrigerator filled with milk for our coffee and snacks. I loved this place, and the thought of losing it filled me with as much anger as dread. I was committed to do whatever it took to assure its survival.

So, two weeks after my conversation with Wilcox, I found myself sitting in the conference room. I had decided to meet with the magician and was about to share the news, as well as the reason for my decision, with my team.

They entered the conference room, unsure of what to expect, as we did not, as a matter of practice, have many agendaless meetings. "As many of you know," I said quietly but sternly, "business is down, we are not making the numbers we need, and, to be frank, a lot of you are not happy."

The faces around the room told me that my colleagues were terrified that their worst fears were about to be realized. A few looked like they were holding back tears, including my key salesman.

This forced me to get to the point quickly. "I am going to seek help," I blurted out. Now the group looked at me in a funny kind of way, as if I were heading into rehab.

"What I mean is that I . . . we . . . all of us, need to change."
As the words stumbled out, I realized this was still heading in
the wrong direction.

OK, I thought, time to fess up. "Look, I think you are some
of the most talented people I have ever worked with. Our
product is terrific. We have a brand name that is respected
and loved. But the world of business is changing and getting
tougher. We have to change to enjoy future success. But we
cannot do it alone. We are too used to doing things our own
way, and we don't stray outside our comfort level. We need
some kind of catalyst that will help us think differently. And I
believe I have found the guy to do it."

Everyone was relieved that they still had their jobs and that
we were moving forward. I told them how this "consultant"
helped Wilcox turn his business around and about the success
it generated. We talked about our present difficulties, how
the industry was changing, and the day-to-day frustrations we
faced. My openness seemed to knock down a wall of defen-
siveness, and everyone agreed that we needed some outside
thinking and new ideas. Then they wanted to know when the
"consultant" would start.

"Soon," I told them. I didn't bother to tell them George
Miles's trade. I was hoping to keep it secret, at least until I
actually met him and saw him do his "magic." Heading back
to my office, I immediately picked up the phone to make the
appointment. If I waited even five minutes more, I thought, I
might chicken out.

I got the magician's voice mail. "Afis-gafifis, I've disappeared again. Leave a message. If you're calling for a lesson,
pick a time and date—any time and date. I'll let you know if
you picked the right one."

I kept waiting for a sign-off or beep. Later I learned that
is one of his trademarks. He never says anything final like

good-bye. Apparently, a prominent magic magazine incorrectly reported his death. He spent weeks explaining to people that he was still around. After that he became superstitious about his mortality. He figured if he never said good-bye, he'd live forever.

I spoke into the silence on the phone: "This is Jonathan West. I am interested in a lesson and was referred by Wilcox. I'm free to meet on Thursday at 10 A.M. Please let me know if that works."

I hung up, wondering if I should just send Wilcox his check back and forget the whole thing.

THINK DIFFERENTLY— FOLLOW THE OTHER HAND

The magician called my office around 1 p.m. and left a message.

"Smart kid," he said. "You picked the right time and date. Go to the corner of Eighth Avenue and Thirty-fourth Street. That's in New York City! You'll see the sign for my shop."

End of message. I pictured the cross streets he mentioned. This was a part of town I didn't spend much time in, an eclectic part of Manhattan that connects you with Macy's, Madison Square Garden, and the New Yorker Hotel, the fabled headquarters of the "Moonies." Entering a nondescript building, I climbed three flights up a rickety staircase and entered the only door on the floor.

Inside was a world that was completely foreign to me, but also one that I would very quickly get to know. Waist-high glass counters spanned three sides of the room. They were filled with the most mystical assortments of magic paraphernalia that would serve me well in my tutelage: large, brightly colored silks (I learned later to call them foulards) that could disappear or change colors on command, giant silver balls that floated in the air, jumbo cards, magic wands, old-fashioned top hats, floating lightbulbs, candles that turned into dancing canes, and real silver dollars that squeezed through the thin neck of a soda bottle. Each trick had a name that was as mysterious as its effect: the Professor's Nightmare, Chinese Linking Rings, Phantom Tubes, Die Boxes, Square Circles, Foo Cans, Chop-Chop Cups, and the Passe-Passe bottles. Would my colleagues suggest I take medical leave when I told them where I'd gone?

When I wasn't busy looking down into the glass cases, I found myself gazing up at the wall-to-wall photos of magicians in tails and hats, clown suits, and flamingo outfits. Many of these magicians were doing the most uncanny things to their assistants—shoving swords through them, cutting them in half, levitating them in the air, turning their heads 360 degrees, and making their bodies zigzag in impossible positions. Others showed a peculiar-looking bald-headed guy meeting with famous people, like the photos you sometimes see in people's offices. He was shaking hands with the usual suspects: the mayor of New York, the President of the United States, and players from the New York Yankees.

And then I saw him, in the flesh. Behind the counter stood a man of average height, broad shoulders, round face, bulbous nose, and shiny bald head—with one long hair wrapped around many times as if to hide his baldness. (I later learned that he still went to the barber for a "hair cut.")

His suit was rumpled. His shirt was stained. His tie undone and his fly partially unzipped. Since I was the only one in the shop, I assumed he was embarrassed by his sloppy dress because when he spotted me, he quickly went into a back room to tidy up. Minutes later, he came out; the suit was still rumpled, shirt was still stained, the zipper still down. The only change was that his tie was pushed into a neat knot.

Before I could walk over to introduce myself, George Miles called out as if he were singling me out in a standing-room-only crowd, "Hey, kid, want to see a trick?"

It really was not a question, because he didn't wait for an answer. Instead, he pulled out a flattened top hat, made in the days when top hats were constructed to pop up and down with the flick of a wrist. Popping open the hat, he turned the bottom toward me and asked me if anything was inside. "No," I said.

"Phantasmagoria! You're one heck of a smart kid," he replied.

The magician showed me a black and white die, about three inches high, which he placed in the hat. Then he brought out a fire engine–red box the size of a tissue box. It had four doors: two on top and two in the front. The pair of doors on top opened upward; the doors on the front opened side by side, on the side facing me. When all four were open, you could see right into the interior of the box.

"What's in the box?" he asked, as he opened all four of its doors.

"Nothing," I responded.

"You're pure genius," he remarked with a smile.

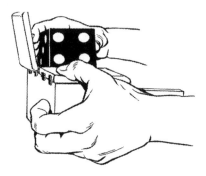

The magician plucked the die out of the hat and placed it in the right side of the box. The die completely filled the space. Then he shut all the doors. "Did you see what just happened? The die disappeared," he remarked.

"No, it's on the right side of the box," I emphatically reminded him.

And, in fact, as I pointed to the right side, he tilted the box to the left. I heard a loud, audible "clunk" as the die slid to the other side.

"Bongo-Mongo! I hate to tell you you're wrong, kid," he said as he proudly opened the door on the right side. Nothing was there.

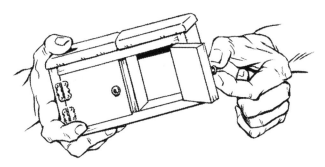

"It's on the left side," I quickly replied. Now he tilted the box to the right and with a loud stamp of his foot (probably to hide the clunk the die made as it slid over) he proudly opened the left door to show me that nothing was there.

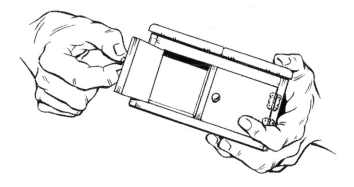

"It's on the right!" I screamed out. He responded by sliding the box in the opposite direction. A "clunk" sound followed.

"There's absolutely nothing inside," he assured me as he opened the right door.

I was feeling a variety of different emotions at this time—embarrassment, frustration, and anger. It was obvious how the trick was done. It was obvious that this guy, George Miles, was a lousy magician. It was obvious that I was wasting my time and that Wilcox was going to have his check cashed without my even completing the first visit. As if reading my mind, the magician opened all the doors of the box at the same time. The box was empty. The die was gone. He reached into the hat, which had been by my side the whole time, and took out the die.

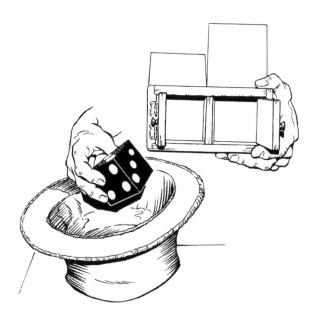

"Lesson number one has begun," he said. "Before we continue, why don't you call me by my trade name, Merlin."

"OK, Merlin," I repeated. Satisfied with my acknowledgment of his professional standing, Merlin began to teach.

"Magic is the art of understanding human behavior and the assumptions we make," he explained. "My role is to have you follow the wrong assumptions with the result of mystifying you."

To demonstrate, he pulled out the red box. "What I placed into the box may or may not have been the die. But you assumed it was." Merlin smiled. "Based on that, I knew that when I tilted the box and you heard the clunking sound you would assume that the die was moving from one compartment to the next. I knew you assumed that when I coughed or thumped my foot I was covering up for the sound. In essence, you were the one making the magic happen by forming the wrong assumptions. I just directed you there. The accepted term for this is mis-di-rec-tion," Merlin said theatrically.

"But there is another school of thought that my compeer, Marc DeSouza, likes to remind me of—mis-di-rec-tion is a misnomer. Marc, a successful real-estate developer and head of the ethics committee for the Society of American Magicians, points out that the magician is actually directing you, not misdirecting you, to follow those assumptions.

"I am directing where you focus your attention with the result of providing 'magic'—a form of harmless entertainment that puts a smile on people's faces, creates awe, and leaves you with an experience you never forget.

"But in business and in life, we are up against forces within ourselves and outside our control that are directing us to look in a particular direction that forms our assumptions. We often treat these assumptions as truths rather than a set of beliefs.

"We frantically search the house looking for the keys we assume are lost, when they are actually in our hands. We assume the person sitting next to us at a party doesn't care for us because she is neither talkative nor smiling, when in fact she is a wonderful, caring person who is merely very shy. In situations like these, we fool ourselves, and in most cases the consequences of doing so are harmless. Other times, they are not.

"What assumptions did IBM make when they let Bill Gates license his operating system, rather than just purchase it outright?" asked Merlin. "Microsoft may not have been the company it is today.

"AT&T had the same information on the future of cellular technology as their competitors had, yet they passed on investing in this business, following the direction of thinking that cellular service was always going to be local. Making an assumption like that is one of the reasons AT&T was purchased by another telecommunications company it once owned," he continued.

"Think about how Coke felt when they assumed that taste is everything. The masters at building an emotional relationship with the consumer never bothered to do a real test of 'New' versus 'Old' Coke. Instead, they assumed that blind tasting indicated people preferred the new taste to the old. These are classic cases of focusing in the wrong direction," said Merlin.

"But understanding the principles of directing attention opens a whole new world of successful opportunities for marketing and business solutions."

I was baffled and wondered where this was leading, afraid he was going to suggest misleading clients to get ahead. Reading my mind once again, Merlin said, "What I am now going to show you is no foola-doola. Watch closely.

"I am going to take the coin from my left hand and hold it in my right."

I followed his actions like a beagle following the scent of a criminal. One minute he was holding the coin in his left hand, and then it was gone and inside the fist of the right hand.

"So let's see if you've got the focus-pocus to answer my next question," said Merlin with a wicked grin. "Your brain and all your life experiences tell you that the coin is in my right hand.

"I can tell you're making that assumption because your eyes are looking at the right hand holding the coin.

"But what if you were to challenge that assumption? What if you opposed what your present intellect was telling you? What if you stopped and considered that the coin may not be in the right hand? What conclusion might you draw?" Merlin said in a way that invited response.

"I'd say the coin never left the left hand and you are holding it, even though your left hand appears empty," I replied.

"Exactamundo!" exclaimed Merlin, as he opened his right hand to reveal an empty palm. Then he directed my attention to his left hand holding the coin. "By challenging your assumption, you have discovered the secret to the trick and a new solution that did not exist for you before."

I felt a sense of accomplishment and recognized a feeling that I was on an exciting journey down a river of new possibilities.

"Mis-di-rec-tion," exclaimed Merlin, "is not only a method for achieving magic. It is a reminder of a simple question that we must constantly ask ourselves, or else be willing to accept the consequences if we don't. Which hand do we choose? Do we follow what everyone else is thinking or do we challenge their assumptions and look in the other hand for new ideas? Some people see this need to constantly question as a burden. Foola-boola on them. Deciding which hand to follow is your opportunity to uncover real solutions. It's also the fastest way of creating new ideas, as well as the most crucial step in creating your own magic.

"That is the lesson for today: When you are looking for a new business solution, don't assume and follow everyone else's lead. Instead, *follow the other hand.* Thinking about cutting costs to increase profits? Maybe you should be considering raising prices. This will force you to challenge the assumption, which leads you to find new solutions."

Merlin then handed me a sheet of blank paper. "I want you to write one very big goal that you would like to accomplish next year," he said. "Don't worry about whether it's realistic or not. Just write it down."

I thought for a second and wrote down, "Make the supermarkets demand my products."

"Now," said Merlin, "write down all the reasons why that will not happen."

This was all too easy to do. I made a list:

1. Too many competing products to choose from.
2. No leverage.
3. Competitors constantly cutting price.
4. Customers don't care who imports the product when the product still appears the same. (Olive oil is olive oil.)
5. Competitors offer supermarkets more money to get shelf space.
6. Technology is allowing the supermarkets and gourmet shops to go directly to my sources.
7. We have limited control over the pricing of an item that we don't manufacture.

Merlin looked over my shoulder and sighed. "Holy moly, I can see your dilemma," he said with great empathy. "You're in an impossible situation. Perhaps the best advice I can give to you is to sell the business now. Take the money. Retire comfortably. Let some other sucker fail. At least it won't be you."

At first I thought he was kidding, but the look in his eye told me he was serious. Now I was furious. Who was he to tell me to chuck generations of sweat, hard work, and dedication, not just from my family but from all the people who worked for us? This wasn't advice, this was an insult, and I plunged my hand into my pocket to pull out Wilcox's check and to keep me from using it to hit Merlin in the jaw. As if reading my mind Merlin said, "Before you knock me on the floor I want you to grab that piece of paper you just wrote on, crumple it in a tight, tight ball, and hold it in your left hand above your head. Do it now!" he commanded.

I did as he instructed. I crumpled that paper like I was crushing the face of the enemy and a little of Merlin's at the same time. In a tight fist I held the paper above my head. I felt both a little better and foolish at the same time.

"Now," said Merlin in the same commanding voice, "take this blank piece of paper and write down all the ways you can *make the supermarkets demand your products.* Don't edit. Don't judge. Just challenge all the reasons you are holding in your left hand."

It wasn't easy at first. As I began to think of ideas, I would immediately begin to discount them as impossible. Forcing myself not to listen to those voices chanting "it can't be done," I began to make my list:

1. Supply products that my competition doesn't have and that cannot be found anywhere else.
2. Use my knowledge of the industry that the supermarkets don't have.
3. Use my personal connections with my suppliers that the supermarkets don't have.
4. Help the smaller gourmet shops grow.
5. Stop thinking like the middleman and act more like the distributor.
6. Begin competing with my buyers—large and small.

"Stop here," said Merlin. "Tell me, how do you feel right now?"

I answered him without thinking. "I feel like I just entered through a doorway that's always been there but I hadn't seen before. It's not that I haven't thought about doing some of these things. But for some reason they feel more doable, more real."

"Good." Merlin smiled. "That's the result of empowering yourself by challenging the 'experts,' even if one of the experts is yourself. How's your energy?"

"Pretty good. I mean, my answers came a lot faster than I expected. Each idea felt like it was feeding the fire, burning brighter with each addition." I stopped there, feeling a little embarrassed by my poetic imagery.

"You've taken the first step in following the other hand. I want you to take the list back to your group. Explain the process you went through and then ask them to consider which hand they want to follow. They will resist the process at first, so here's what I suggest. Take the first item on your list—supply products your competition doesn't have—and let them suggest how that can be accomplished."

"Are you kidding?" I said. "I am excited by the idea of having something no one else has, but I am also a realist. This can't be done."

"Are you deciding not to look at the other hand?" kidded Merlin. "Take a minute and think like a magician! Let me explain.

"Magic is first created in the mind of the magician: What if I could make an object float in mid-air? What if I could push a needle through a balloon without it bursting? What if I could walk through a brick wall? In other words, magic begins by us choosing what we want to accomplish first, without worrying about how to achieve it. This is called the *effect*. If we wondered how to accomplish a trick before we chose an effect, there would very little magic in this world.

"Bill Smith, a master at building illusions for the world's greatest magicians, provided this illustration," said Merlin. "Bill said:

> *Rick Thomas, a well-known illusionist, wanted to do a trick in which he changed an adult tiger into a baby tiger. Rick brought that effect to the table. Then Jim Steinmeyer, one of today's greatest designers of illusions, got together with us. Within half an hour, Jim figured out the method. We built it, and two weeks later Rick was performing the illusion.*

"I must point out," said Merlin, "and I am sure Bill Smith would agree, that most great effects take longer than that to develop. I must also bring to your attention that choosing an effect and then achieving it doesn't guarantee success. It must be relevant to the audience.

"I know a magician who mastered the incredible effect of making four silver dollars cascade down the fingers of his right hand with the end effect of holding a coin between each of his four fingers. Only the most gifted magician can perform this; yet to the layman in the audience the effect feels ordinary and lacks impact.

"John Osher, a successful entrepreneur who I will talk about in another lesson, once noted that the magician should never focus on wanting to make the effect happen at the expense of figuring out what to do with it. John owns a space-age two-wheeled electric vehicle that makes it fun to get around.

"According to John, 'It's an amazing technology that hasn't really found its purpose. This vehicle represents a typical situation where the inventor gets overly infatuated with the magic of what he's achieved physically and is really not well connected to the market. It's not relevant to enough audiences.'"

Merlin continued, "OK, let's now pick an effect—say I want to create a strong visual that is easy to see in a large audience using something I am wearing—making my tie rise in the air upon command fits the bill. Now I *decide which hand to follow*. The 'left hand' says that a tie cannot seemingly rise on its own, so we then challenge that assumption and look at what solution can be held in the 'right hand':

1. Employ magnets of opposite polarity that are concealed in the tie and in my hand.
2. Use wires built into the tie in a way that cannot be detected.
3. Create a tie that appears to be cloth but is actually a helium balloon.

"Once I empower myself to make the seemingly impossible possible by challenging assumptions, creative solutions seem to multiply as fast as rabbits.

"My next step is to explore the *method* for achieving the effect of making the tie rise. Let's say I choose to focus on using wires. I will try different strengths and lengths. I will explore various shapes—straight, zigzag, or round. I will play with different types of ties. I will invent ways of hiding the wires from the audience's sight.

"Once the effect and method are determined, my energies are spent developing a *performance*—the execution of the trick. I know you have been admiring the tie I am wearing ever since you entered this shop."

I wanted to tell Merlin that it was his style of dress that I noticed, but he didn't give me a chance to respond.

"This tie was given to me by the Great Andini—the greatest levitation artist of all time. He could make anything float in the air—cars, elephants, and, most miraculously, ties!"

Suddenly, Merlin's tie began to rise away from his body and into the air. His hands were at his sides the whole time. Just as suddenly, it fell back into place.

"I won't reveal the secret of the trick, but I have given you the process and enough hints to figure out how it is accomplished."

I was dying to know the secret of the rising tie and felt frustrated at having to figure it out myself. Sensing this, Merlin continued.

"It's perfectly natural to want to know how a trick is done. During our lessons, I sometimes will explain all. Other times, you will be challenged to figure out the solutions yourself. Like how the tie rises. But when it comes to business 'secrets,' I will hold nothing back. You see, I have a passion for how business thinks.

"A lot of successful businesspeople love magic, and many have walked up the same steps as you. In between selling or teaching these people magic, I ask about their businesses and day-to-day challenges. Discussion follows and I often end up challenging their thinking and providing insights that turn into solutions they employ. Between having these conversations and staying up with the business trades, I've gained a lot of knowledge. Some of it's proprietary. Luckily, there's a lot I can share with you. Did you hear the joke about the scientist who invented a new deodorant called Invisible?" Merlin smiled. "You rub it on and disappear, leaving everyone wondering where the smell is coming from."

In absence of a belly laugh from me, he continued.

"In the deodorant business, there was another joke called body sprays. All across the globe, people used body sprays to deal with body odor, except in the United States. Perhaps it's our obsession with taking baths and showers, but the category of body sprays did not exist. According to many marketing experts, Americans only cared about their armpits and eliminating sweat and smell. They assumed the U.S. market for body sprays did not exist.

"Unilever chose an effect—selling a body spray, called AXE, to the U.S. market. In deciding to follow the other hand, the company challenged the assumptions of the category leaders like Sure and Right Guard who focused on telling the consumer that their products eliminated 'sweat and smell.' By looking at the other hand, they saw a new market that didn't care about how they smelled as much as they cared about helping 18- to 24-year-old guys 'get the girl.' They explored many methods that would accomplish the effect and chose one—messages that communicated AXE to these guys as a spray that attracts the girls of their dreams. Unilever then chose multiple numbers of performances to execute the method. Web banners displayed humorous scenarios of cheerleaders chasing football players across the field. In stores, TV commercials at Wal-Mart showed a guy (who has just used AXE) being kissed by a complete stranger standing beside him at the checkout. Instead of just selling AXE in the expected aisle along with the other deodorants, they placed the product where the customers were: the electronic, music, and auto departments of Wal-Mart and other retail distributors.

"The *performance* of AXE did the trick. Unilever defied the experts and created a business in the U.S. market where a business did not exist. AXE became the number-one-selling new product in its category the year it was launched. Within two years, their competitors launched their own body sprays and are still playing catch-up."

Suddenly it clicked.

Great-great-grandpa had rules, and those rules were passed along from generation to generation; no one questioned them, mainly because they worked. Rule #1: Never compete with your buyers—they are the hands that feed you. Rule #2: Stick with what you know best, so you can be the best at it. Rule #3: Stay in the middle—then you can make money from either side.

If the family was to survive and thrive, I'd have to challenge the "family rules" and see what new solutions lie in the other hand.

I shared this with Merlin and then said, "If I look at the same hand as my great-great-grandfather, I see a company servicing both suppliers and purchasers. In essence, we are a service business that is only as good as our last sale and dependent upon relationships built over time. If I challenge that assumption and look at the list I made up, I see us as experts in olive oil, olives, and related gourmet foods. No one knows about pricing, sourcing, and distributing these goods as much as we do. This has to provide us with an advantage and opportunity."

Merlin beamed and suggested I present this to my team, followed by exploring the first challenge I wrote down. He even gave me a checklist to hand out to the group summarizing how the whole process works.

CHECKLIST FOR LESSON #1

Think Differently—
Follow the Other Hand

1. Create an effect. Deodorant manufacturers believed that a body spray would never succeed in the United States because the category simply did not exist. But they were just looking at one hand. They failed to imagine what might be in the other hand and instead stuck to the conventional wisdom.

2. Follow the other hand. Unilever, the manufacturer of AXE, looked at the other hand and challenged this assumption. They challenged the view that the main reason people buy deodorants is to avoid sweat and smell. AXE accepted that (a) the fact that no one had done a body spray in the United States did not mean it was impossible and (b) guys don't care how they smell when with other guys, but with girls it's a different story. Unilever decided to position the body spray to guys aged 18 to 24 as a way of helping them "get the girl."

3. Develop the method. Try thinking what the process would be if you followed the new solutions or ideas. What could you accomplish if you chose to ignore those voices that said, "It can't be done"? What if it could be done?

4. Begin with a great performance. AXE tested provocative banner advertising such as showing cheerleaders running after football players and trying to pull their pants down. One million visitors clicked on the ad, visited the site, and stayed, on average, more than five minutes. This was a month before the product was even in the stores. Unilever also placed AXE where the guys shopped in the store: the electronic, music, and auto departments of Wal-Mart and other retail distributors.

5. Achieving the effect. Following the other hand generates new ideas and offers great success, and the rewards go to those who perform first. AXE was one of the most successful product launches in 2002. The product line was expanded to more than sixteen similar body sprays from

Apollo to Voodoo. Within two years, their competitors introduced their own body sprays, closely mimicking AXE's original positioning. AXE was first to challenge the assumption, and the others have been playing catch-up ever since.

Before I left to go back to the office, Merlin told me about a discussion he had with Nick Pudar, Vice President of Planning and Business Development at OnStar. Nick loves magic and often discusses the relationship between magic and business.

"OnStar is a business created by GM," Nick had told Merlin. "It's a totally innovative communications service that has changed the way we think about cars and the experience of driving them. In the year 2007 approximately four million GM cars will have OnStar subscriptions. OnStar services more than 500,000 calls every month—40,000 calls just to unlock doors. If you are in an accident and your airbag deploys, an OnStar advisor will automatically contact the police. Several other car companies have subcontracted with OnStar for their own customers. OnStar has saved hundreds of lives. But the business almost never happened."

According to Nick, "In the early nineties, Rick Wagoner, then the president of GM North America, believed that the future of the auto industry went beyond fast, efficiently run, and comfortable cars and chose an *effect*: developing a new type of communications system for the car.

"The overall obstacles in launching this kind of product were significant. At the time OnStar was conceived, the typical total life cycle of a vehicle program was eight to ten years. It took two years to create the product, two years to test and integrate it into the manufacturing processes, and then four to six years of having the hardware built into the vehicles as part of the regular production run. Heavily integrated technologies such as the electronics represented by OnStar traditionally would need to wait many years for the next major redesign of the total vehicle. Only then would you see opportunities to implement major improvements. In contrast, the average electronic product development cycle, like OnStar technology, was eighteen months. It was initially assumed that these two product cycles were incompatible. So the first thing GM had to do was follow the other hand, by acknowledging this assumption and assessing if it was true or just a set of beliefs. Even Chet Huber, who was there in the beginning and is now president of OnStar, said that it would have been easy to walk away from the project. Nobody really wanted to challenge the assumption.

"Luckily, someone did," said Nick. "Rick Wagoner empowered the team to 'follow the other hand.' The method used was simply breaking all the product development rules, and through diligent engineering studying and identifying the absolute latest integration point in the existing processes. That was coupled with a strong attention to detail, and they got it right. Two years later, the first OnStar unit was launched. That was in 1997. OnStar continued to test this assumption; within five years of the launch they had instituted eight generations of technology updates.

"There's another moral to this story," Nick suggested. "By showing that different development cycles are compatible, GM was able to integrate satellite-radio systems in our cars faster than the competition," Nick told Merlin. "By the end of 2005, GM offered three million satellite-radio units. All other car companies combined only had a little over 1.5 million—and that was dominated by Honda."

"Obviously, following the other hand can give you a competitive advantage through new ideas and, thus, transform your business," said Merlin. I nodded my head in agreement. "Looks like you're ready for lesson number two—how to get your customers to buy a product before they even pull out their credit card.

"But first I have something for you to give to your team. It's a form of power," Merlin said very seriously. "When I do close-up magic I can often read the skepticism in a participant's face. A very effective saying that I use in my magic, I learned from Slydini, one of the greatest close-up artists ever. He taught me the power of speaking the truth. If you are nervous, tell the audience you are nervous—and everyone relaxes, including you. When you see skepticism, say, 'I can see in your eyes that you do not believe me.' It always makes the participant smile, because that is exactly what they are thinking.

"But words are not enough. For example, if you say you have two coins in your hand and they don't believe you, you must open your hand or jingle them in your fist—they must experience the proof. We will talk about the power of the experience in great length in another lesson.

"For now, when you go back to your team, it's important that they go through the experience of challenging assumptions themselves. You're going to perform a card trick entitled 'Impossible,' and your group will figure out the solution to the trick."

I looked at Merlin in amazement as I thought to myself, How is my team going to accomplish that?

Reading my mind, Merlin continued, "Just like you are going to do now!"

Merlin performed "Impossible" three times. Each time I was convinced I had just seen the impossible happen. Then he put the cards in his right hand and asked me to decide which hand to follow. This forced me to challenge my assumptions. I came up with five ideas, narrowed it to two, then one. I shared my solution with Merlin.

"You are correct!" said Merlin. "How do you feel?"

"Like I could conquer the world," I beamed.

"That's the energy that erupts when you empower yourself to think differently. You're going to perform 'Impossible' several times, then invite the team to challenge their assumptions and work together to figure out the solution to the trick. Just like you did, they will! Then you will reveal the secret, and they will have had a positive experience of what it's like to decide which hand to follow. Once that happens, the ideas will flow.

"But before you engage your group in following assumptions using magic as metaphor, you must establish your own expertise in magic." Merlin then pulled out the magic die box, revealed its secret, explained the presentation, provided me with a simple routine that was easy to learn and perform, and instructed me what to say when asked how I did the trick.

It was typical of Merlin to change gears. He suddenly asked me to take one of the pages from my notepad, tear it into five pieces, and write a different store address he recited on each piece. The locations included Midtown, Brooklyn, Queens, Soho, and Greenwich Village. Once done, I was instructed to fold those pieces and spread them out in any order on the table. Next, I was asked to point to any three of the five pieces of paper. Then two of the three remaining. Then just one.

"Pick up the paper you chose," said Merlin very nonchalantly, "and meet me at that store's address next week, 11:00. Don't forget to take the rest of the folded papers home with you and toss them out."

"You'll know where to meet me?" I asked nervously.

"We'll find out." Merlin smiled as he ushered me out the door.

MAGIC TRICK #1

Impossible—The Power of Assumptions

The trick is also called the "Two Card Monte" by many magicians. It works because the participant assumes you are using two different cards. The two cards needed can be purchased in any of the magic shops listed in the back of this book. Or you can request a free set of cards, by hitting the contact button on *andycohen.com* and include you mailing address.

Effect: Two cards are shown. One is face up; the other face down. The cards magically switch places.

Method: The secret is in the cards. They are double sided. One card has the seven of hearts on one side and the ace of spades on the other. The second card has a red back on both sides. You begin by holding a card in each hand and flicking the two cards against each other (demonstrating that there are only two cards).

You then place the two cards in your right hand in a spread condition (use your left hand if you are a lefty). The top card should be spread to the right.

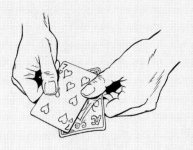

Turn your wrist, to show the other sides of the cards. As the hand turns, use your right thumb to pull the top card to the left, while the fingers push the lower card to the right. The illusion of two "normal" cards is maintained.

Repeat this once or twice. The participant will see a seven of hearts and an ace of spades with red backs. The effect will be that when they see the seven of hearts facing up, they will assume the ace of spades is facing down and vice versa. Remove the face-up card (let's say the ace of spades) and hold it next to the participant's ear. Then ask them to name the card you are holding face down. They will say the seven of hearts. Flip the ace of spades over secretly and silently, then pull your hand back into view to show them that you are holding the seven of hearts in your other hand.

Go back to the beginning move and repeat. (But not more than three times as it increases the odds of the participant asking to see the cards.)

Performance: (Pull out the two cards and flick them against each other. Then begin.)

"I have never had to testify in a court of law. Yet I always wondered what kind of witness I would be."

(As you talk, put the two cards together and flip them over as described in the method section so that the participant sees both sides.)

"If I had to testify that I saw the accused leave a party that I had attended, could I be absolutely certain they had left? I am not sure. What card is this?" (Hold out the ace of spades in one hand and the red back card in the other. The participant will say, "Ace of spades.")

"Suppose the ace of spades stepped out of the room." (Place the ace of spades behind the participant's head, just next to the ear.) "Who would be left in the room?"

(The participant will say, "The seven of hearts.")

"I think you are confused; it cannot be. You see, the seven of hearts is here." (Pull back the card from behind the participant's head and show the seven of hearts.) "It's not easy being a witness. Is it?"

(Put the cards together and repeat. Take your bow.)

As soon as I got back to the office I sent an e-mail to my executive team, asking everyone to meet in the conference room the following day. This team of six people not only oversaw the thirty-six employees that run the business, they ran my life! Before we go further, I think it would be fair to tell you a little about them. I'll take them one by one.

BUDDY, SALES

How can you not like a guy named Buddy? He grew up on the streets of the Bronx with seven brothers and sisters and took care of five of them when his parents had to work. At the same time he put himself through college, where he graduated with honors. His playing field in his youth was the streets of New York, and it made him one of the most competitive people I know. It's been suggested that he play on both teams during the annual company baseball game. He is a great salesman with an intuitive sense of what motivates people to act. Yet when he gets an idea, he doesn't distinguish between a good idea and a bad one—he's just determined to push the idea through. When it comes to asking the group for new thinking, I have to be careful with Buddy.

THELMA, FINANCE

This woman is tough. She answers the phone with one word, "Thelma." She never says more than a few words at a time. Thelma treats a penny like a dollar, a dollar like a hundred dollars, and anything over a hundred dollars like gold. A stone bleeds more than Thelma. Yet she's one of the funniest people you'll ever meet and has a way of making others laugh, as long as the topic isn't about increasing spending. She is also a sports fanatic, dedicated to assembling and organizing the company's pool for football, baseball, hockey, soccer, curling, and even the national dart competition. As far as turning to Thelma for an idea, forget it; she doesn't have a creative bone in her body.

CHIEF, ACCOUNT MANAGEMENT

His real name is Brian W. Wilson. No one knows why he's called Chief. Seniority or wisdom isn't the reason, since Chief is only a few years out of college. He's underpaid, overworked, and handles more responsibility than his experience dictates. Yet I will take Chief over some of the more experienced account people. Chief's secret is that he likes people. Period. Harmony is everything to him. So is fairness. He will never roll over for a client just to make them happy; instead he looks for the compromise that is fair and right for all. Perhaps this explains the premature thinning of his hair and his ability to see both sides of a problem. The others don't know it, but he's the first one I go to when I need someone to bounce an idea off of.

SUNJAY, IT

He loves to fix things: phones, leaky faucets in the company kitchen, and, most important, computers. He's cranky all the time because of the constant demands to help download a software program, get a frozen computer operational again, insert digital images into a PowerPoint presentation, and sometimes just turn the computer on. To Sunjay, we are all computer dummies, because we are constantly asking for his help, particularly with the same old problems. In fairness, we act that way because Sunjay hates explaining how things are done. It's faster if he fixes the problem himself. Collaboration isn't his strength, especially when we brainstorm on important issues.

DEBORAH, GENERAL MANAGER

She's as dependable as a Swiss clock, fair with all of us, and never stops working until a problem is solved. Unfortunately, the problem can go on too long. When faced with a decision, Deborah pulls out the yellow pad, draws a line down the middle, identifies the pros and cons, and then attempts to have all of us address every issue. This process takes forever; it wears people out and makes us second-guess every move we make. Surprisingly, Deborah is a very talented flute player and artist. She performs in a regional jazz band and also teaches drawing at the local library. She's a great idea person, but only to a point. Once she puts an idea down on a piece of yellow paper, the spontaneity and energy of the new solution freeze.

SHAWN, HEAD OF LOGISTICS AND DISTRIBUTION

It's ironic that Shawn's choice of career was anything but logical. He was a third-grade science teacher who became an illustrator for a magazine publisher. He began a freelance business on the side doing packaged-goods designs. As an empirical thinker he felt he would be a better illustrator if he also learned about the fulfillment side of the packaged-goods business: how products are shipped and how they end up on the shelves. He discovered there was more money in figuring out how products are manufactured, shipped, and stored on the shelves than in actually making the product more appealing to the customers. Besides, being on the creative side means having to deal with people; Shawn would rather deal with crates, pallets, and scanning codes. He's honest, hardworking, and has the antennae to spot problems before they happen. Yet this makes him difficult to work with because he's the first to point out why something won't work rather than be supportive about why it will.

A s I walked into the conference room, I was buzzing with new energy and new ideas, but also very concerned about the group's reaction to Merlin and his lesson. That concern was reinforced when I found my team sitting quietly around the conference table. In the center of the table was an eleven-piece Amazing Magic Trick kit, a fake bunny, and a cheap plastic top hat.

It turned out that Wilcox's son and Buddy's son played soccer on the same team. During a weekend game, the two got into a conversation and realized they both knew me. Wilcox assumed I had shared the "consultant's" background and let the "rabbit" slip out of the hat. Buddy, in turn, let the word out to everyone, and I was about to help my team challenge their first assumptions about our new "consultant."

I was all set to take Merlin's advice and establish my own "expertise" in magic. But first I picked up the rabbit, petted it, and gave it to Thelma with instructions to feed it every day. We all laughed. Then I pulled out the die box and began performing, using the plastic hat as my prop.

I was so nervous doing the trick that it added to the effect, and the group was truly embarrassed that I was giving the secret away. You can imagine their reaction when the die was not to be found in the box and reappeared in the hat.

"Unbelievable," said Deborah, the general manager. "I was positive that you were sliding the die back and forth."

"I saw you put the die in the box," Sunjay, head of technology, said, "then it disappeared. Impossible!"

"It's just a trick," Shawn, the logistics guy, said with a shrug of his shoulders.

"Some trick. One minute I was embarrassed for you," confided Buddy, the sales director, "now I am the one embarrassed. By the way, how did you do it?"

Merlin had prepared me for this and I answered, "I did it extremely well." Then, as Merlin had instructed, I quickly put the trick away to prevent anyone from examining the box. Instead, I jumped right into the concept of "mis-di-rec-tion" and deciding "which hand to follow." I noticed that no one was questioning that the source of this discussion was a magician.

Chief, the account manager, grasped the concept immediately. "I am constantly putting out fires while facing a barrage of important issues. The only way to survive is to depend on my assumptions to help me make quick decisions, even as they relate to long-term strategies. For example, I nixed Sunjay's recommendation to purchase a costly software program based on what I believed. I didn't even bother reading the details he provided me. A few days later, when I had some downtime, I glanced at the document Sunjay prepared about the application and the benefits for servicing clients. It completely contradicted the information on which I had based my decision. I had a follow-up discussion with Sunjay, and we are going with his recommendation."

"Which will save us a lot of money after the first year," Sunjay piped in.

"Boy, did I misdirect myself," admitted Chief.

This seemed the appropriate time to demonstrate the "Impossible" trick Merlin had shown me. I pulled out two cards, a red back card and a seven of hearts. I flipped them over to show a red back card and an ace of spades.

"I have never had to testify in a court of law. Yet I always wondered what kind of witness I would be," I chattered.

As I talked I flipped the two cards over so that everyone could see both sides.

"If I had to testify that I saw the accused leave a party that I had attended, could I be absolutely certain they had left? I am not sure.

"Deborah, what card is this?" I held out the ace of spades in one hand and the red back card in the other.

"The ace of spades," said Deborah with a look that said it was obvious.

"Suppose the ace of spades stepped out of the room," I said as I placed the ace of spades behind her head. "Which card would be left in the room?"

Deborah looked at the face-down card and said: "The seven of hearts."

"Deborah, I think you are confused," I said. "It cannot be. The seven of hearts is here." As I said this, I pulled back the card from behind Deborah's head and showed her the seven of hearts.

"That's impossible," Deborah cried out.

I repeated the trick for both Buddy and Thelma and received the same reaction. Then I told the team that they were now going to figure out themselves how it was done.

"Impossible," repeated Deborah. "I can never figure out magic tricks."

"You will now. I'd like everyone to call out his or her assumptions on how the trick was done and I'll write them on the whiteboard."

At first no one said anything. Then Buddy yelled out: "Hypnosis...the power of suggestion." I wrote.

Thelma said, "You had three cards and then switched them...somehow." I wrote again.

Sunjay thought for a moment and said: "I believe you only had two cards. But they must not be what they seem." I made another entry on the board.

Chief suggested: "There was a duplicate card hanging on the spectator's back." This went on the board as well.

Deborah looked at the seventeen ideas she had personally written down and suggested the most obvious solution. "I'm guessing you palmed an identical card and then made some kind of switch. But fast, I mean, your hand was only behind my head for a second."

A few more assumptions were suggested. Here's the final list on the conference room whiteboard:

- Hypnosis
- More than two cards
- The two cards are not what they seem to be and are rigged
- There is a duplicate card hanging on the spectator's back
- The magician grabs a different card when the person blinks
- The hand is faster than the eye
- It's impossible to do

We then began to challenge each of these assumptions, quickly eliminating hypnosis, hanging cards on the participant's back, blinking, and impossible to do. (I did the trick again after I had Buddy make a 360-degree turn.)

I then demonstrated that there were only two cards by flicking them against each other. If there were more than two, the others would have been seen. Then I repeated the trick.

Thelma then said, "Trick cards."

Buddy asked, "How can that be?"

Sunjay said: "I assumed they were regular cards because you kept showing us a red back and face card, then red back and a face card. Show us both cards face up at the same time. I bet you can't."

Deborah's eyes lit up. "Jonathan, I never would have expected you to use trick cards. I bet the card with the seven of hearts on one side has the ace of spades on the other!"

"Bingo," I said with a smile as I flipped over the seven of hearts to show the ace of spades on the other side. I then flipped over the red back to show the red back on the other side. Double-sided cards. "I directed you to think one way, and your assumptions led you along. See what happens when you challenge your assumptions and follow the other hand?"

The team beamed with pride. I had a set of cards for everyone and taught them the key components of the trick. The team took their turns performing. We took a lunch break and then were ready to jump back into Merlin's lesson.

You could feel the energy and excitement in the room. Everyone had a lot of questions, and I was glad to have Merlin's checklist. We discussed effect in great detail and touched upon method and performance. Then I decided to put Merlin's lesson to the test. I explained how he had me select an effect and presented it to the group.

"*Make the supermarkets demand my products* is the effect I chose, and here's my list of how we can make it happen," I said. "I am sick and tired of feeling like we have to beg to have the products we represent put on the shelf. I want things on our terms. So, do I hear any ideas on methods for achieving this effect?"

The group went silent. Then Buddy said, "You'd be a real Houdini to pull this off."

"I will give it a try," Deborah quietly volunteered. "Here's my list."

In her usual fashion, Deborah had assembled a mind-numbing twenty ideas. I knew this would get the group off focus and did what Merlin suggested in this type of situation.

"Deborah," I proposed, "what is the one idea on your list that you have never considered before?"

Deborah reacted as if I had insulted her, because she thought all her ideas were original. But then I saw her slowly cross off one idea after another. Finally, she looked up and said almost sheepishly, "I see us making our own product instead of importing it."

Everyone looked at one another. Then Chief jumped in and said, "Why not? Perhaps the market will pay for something we could create ourselves."

Thelma, from finance, who hadn't said a word until now, simply stated, "Too expensive."

Chief, who knew not to argue with Thelma, took another tack by saying, "I mean, we know the cost of goods, we know who makes the best ingredients, we know how to price. If we found the right product, we could produce it cost-effectively." He looked right at Thelma as he said that last part.

Buddy, who thinks every idea is a great one, said, "How about olives stuffed like fortune cookies?"

Sunjay reacted right away. "It's a stupid idea. If it's such a great idea, someone would have done it already."

Once Buddy started, he couldn't be stopped. "Maybe those 'someones' are morons. I say this is a great idea and it belongs on our list. It's a real winner. Best idea so far. Remember, no idea is a stupid one." Then Buddy paused as a thought occurred to him. "Problem is, the oil will make the ink of the fortune run. Sunjay, you think you can work on that?"

Sunjay only rolled his eyes.

Buddy continued with increased enthusiasm. "Hey, here's another blockbuster. How about a line of olives to go with different dressings? Olives from France when you serve French dressing and olives from Italy when you serve Italian dressing?"

"Buddy," I had to interrupt. "We may have a problem getting olives from Russia."

Chief jumped up. "I was wondering, if there are Italian, French, and Russian dressings, how come we don't have American dressing?"

Silence filled the room. I could see their minds at work.

"Hasn't anyone noticed?" asked Shawn, the logistics guy. "Patriotism is becoming overplayed. Besides, I think it's a mistake to take our eyes off our core business."

I wasn't sure if the American dressing idea was great or not, but I knew that Shawn was close to killing the energy that was building up in the room. Thelma, of all people, saved the day and spoke, saying more words in one sentence than I had ever heard her say. "Our best supplier also specializes in New Jersey tomatoes, and that would be a good ingredient for American dressing. I know we can get them cheap," she said with a big smile.

The group was charged and I could feel the energy continue to build as they began to play around with the idea of creating our own product: American dressing. I asked the team if they would continue to think about this idea, meet among themselves, and regroup in two days.

What happened next was no illusion. Seventy-two hours after our last meeting, I walked back into our conference room and did a double take. Pinned up on the wall were sheets of white paper filled with all kinds of scribbles that turned out to be truly original ideas.

In one section of the room was a list of suggested ingredients for the "original" American dressing: juicy, ripe New Jersey tomatoes, chunks of Wisconsin Cheddar, and bits of Virginia ham.

Another section had a more extended list of items: Boston baked beans, New Orleans Creole, Florida orange citrus.

We had generated our own creative electricity by challenging assumptions, and the current was spreading. Thelma had already begun running numbers. Sunjay offered to investigate finding a food scientist to work with—he had a hunch that the science of making a large quantity of dressing was significantly different from that of making a small batch in our office. Buddy was talking to his contacts at the supermarkets to explore the salad dressing category and potential opportunities. Deborah was energized putting her sixty-item list together.

Shawn was energized, too. But his energy went into making a list of all the reasons the American dressing idea wouldn't work.

At this moment the group was enjoying themselves too much to worry if Shawn's attitude was going to be a problem or not. I made a note to talk about this with Merlin. More important, I couldn't wait to share the good news with Merlin, and I made sure to put the address I had chosen into my calendar so I'd be sure to get to my next lesson.

BUILDING TRUST—
MAKING THE
AUDIENCE PART
OF THE ACT

I was feeling a little self-conscious, standing by myself in the Victoria's Secret on Broadway and Prince Street. A man can only look at the lingerie for so long before drawing suspicious glances from the salespeople. Fifteen minutes after our appointed time, Merlin showed up.

"Sorry for running late," he said. His face was flushed, and he had obviously been running. "An associate of mine has a big show tonight and the buzz saw he uses to slice his assistant in two wasn't working properly. That can get sloppy, so I had to help him fix the problem."

I suspected Merlin was really late because he went to some of the other locations and told him so.

"I may be a magician," he smiled, "but I'm not a superman, and the stores you wrote down are scattered all over New York City. And I didn't call the stores asking if you were there either."

"Then how did you know?" I said insistently.

"The same way I know which color nightgown you will select," he said as he scribbled something on a piece of paper and handed it to me folded. We went through the same process as selecting the store address, except this time I pointed at nightgowns. Finally I ended with a blue one.

"What does my prediction say?" Merlin inquired. I looked at the paper and of course it said "blue."

"This is called Magician's Choice, and it's been used for generations to predict a selection," he informed me. "What makes the trick work time after time is that you are given the freedom to make a choice and you believe that the choice is yours. The fact that I control what you will choose is what makes this entertaining, but it does not diminish the message: Trust is established when a consumer believes they have choice and control."

Proving his point, Merlin pulled out a deck of cards, fanned them out, and thrust a card at me that was sticking out from the deck. "Pick a card," he said. When I hesitated he asked, "Don't you trust me?"

I laughed and said that I didn't. It was obvious that he wanted me to pick a specific card, which is called a "force" in magic.

"Do you know that it's impossible to say the words 'belly button' without smiling?" replied Merlin. He had me say the words out loud, and he was right; my lips crept into a small smile.

"Just trying to win back your trust," he said. "Now take the deck and shuffle it until you feel it's impossible for me to know where any one card is within the deck." I did as instructed and handed the deck back to him.

"You know those picture books that you flip through quickly enough that the pictures come together like a movie? I am going to do the same with the deck of cards except they will flash by you slowly. At any time, tell me when to stop, look at the card, and remember it."

Merlin began flipping through the deck at a pace that let me see every card. They were all different. I told him to stop and looked at the queen of spades. There was no way he saw my card, so I was surprised when he handed me the deck and instructed me to shuffle the deck to my heart's content.

"Now do you trust me?" asked Merlin.

"Completely," I said. I meant it. He had let me control when to stop the card and I was sure the choice of card was mine.

"You see, without trust, the magic cannot work," he said. "Think about it—when a magician walks into a room, everyone knows they are going to be fooled in some fashion. Distrust is a magician's occupational hazard.

"Yet somehow a magician overcomes that distrust in the simplest way: You empower the participant, mainly through perceived choice and control. There are other elements as well. You roll up your sleeves when doing a sleight-of-hand trick, or you let the audience test out a razor blade before you pop it in your mouth and swallow it.

"Once trust is established, the seemingly impossible becomes possible, and the result of the magic *feels* real." Merlin then reached into his pocket and handed me a folded piece of paper. Inside it read, "Q of S." Queen of spades. My card.

I was stunned. There was no way he could have known. I immediately wanted to know how he did the trick. But before I could ask he was already answering the question.

"You've got to clock a lot of hours practicing that move,"

Merlin said kindly. "We will save learning that trick for down the road. The lesson to learn is that choice and control requires making a decision and a decision requires energy. Energy can flow in many directions, but when it's channeled in the right direction it begins building a relationship by pulling your customer closer to your product or service.

"The process of building trust also serves another very important purpose," he whispered, as if revealing a secret. "The participant becomes involved in the act."

You can imagine what we looked like, standing among the Victoria's Secret nightgowns—a youngish-looking businessman listening to a balding man dressed in checked pants, a stained white shirt, and a wrinkled overcoat, talking in an animated fashion with a deck of cards in his hands. Finally, a brave salesperson came over and asked if we needed help. Without blinking an eye, Merlin told the salesperson that I was looking for something for my wife, and five minutes later, I walked out of the store $100 poorer than when I first came in.

"That was a lovely choice you made for your wife," said Merlin. "Let's surprise her and send it via FedEx. There happens to be one right around the corner. By the way, say cheese." A flash went off, and Merlin had taken my picture with a tiny digital camera he had produced from his right pocket. Before I could ask why he had photographed me, he grabbed my arm and led me to the FedEx drop-off.

"FedEx and Starbucks have a lot in common," said Merlin.

I told him I didn't see the connection, unless it was that employees of both companies drink a lot of coffee.

"It's obvious," he exclaimed as he pulled out an order form. "Look at all the choices."

Looking at the FedEx form, I realized that he was right. I counted twenty different ways to send a package.

"Starbucks has at least twenty different ways to order as

well," Merlin continued. "Every company needs to think differently at a time when there are more products and services than a consumer can buy. For example, in the old days, free trials were a standard way to stimulate business. Today, everyone is offering free trials, and even if a customer loves the product, there's a good chance they will leave it. There's just too much distance between their first use and next use, too many opportunities to either forget about the product or be offered something better by a competitor."

I sensed he was leading up to an important point and asked, "Is this the beginning of another lesson?"

"Exactamundo," exclaimed Merlin, "so listen up.

"Success in today's business begins by building an emotional relationship with the customer before they actually buy the product or use the service. A simple word for this process is 'trust.' It's the hardest kind of relationship to establish, yet the most binding when it actually does happen. There are three key factors that allow trust to happen: choice, control, and pre-engagement. Let's discuss choice first.

"Choice is about providing options. The newer and more numerous the options, the more powerful the effect in building the relationship. Starbucks first built customer loyalty by providing multiple options for ordering coffee. They also provided options for where to enjoy your purchase: on a sofa, in an armchair, on stools facing the window, or at tables. Starbucks is exploring various entertainment options such as offering DVDs in its retail locations and providing MP3 'fill-ups' that transfer songs onto their customers' portable music players while the barista prepares the order."

I thought about what he was saying, and it reminded me of something that had happened with my son over the weekend. "My son is crazy for the classic song 'Bohemian Rhapsody,' by Queen," I told Merlin, "and he wanted me to use my iTunes account to download the song to his computer. We both enjoyed the downloading process because it was so easy. And I thought to myself, This is what makes iTunes so popular. But now I realize there is another factor that built the consumers' trust with iTunes so fast: choice. The iTunes site provided an array of choices that didn't exist a few years ago. I wasn't locked into buying a whole album for just one song—I could choose and pay for only the songs I wanted. And I could sample dozens of songs in a few minutes."

"You're smarter than Houdini," said Merlin. "So what are your thoughts about control?"

"Aren't choice and control basically the same?"

"No," said Merlin, "choice leads to control." I looked at him. My confusion was apparent. "I take that back. Houdini was smarter," joked Merlin. "Control is providing the consumer with the power to influence behavior or course of events. The best example I can give you is inside this store."

Grabbing me by the arm, Merlin led me into a small deli. Near the cash register, he grabbed a soda for me and ordered a cup of tea for himself.

"Your treat," he mumbled on his way to grab a table in the back of the store. I paid for the soda and tea. When I got to the table, Merlin was sitting down and looking at the bottom of the soda cap that he had just unscrewed.

"Look at this, kid!" he said with the excitement of winning the lottery. "Take a peek under the cap!"

I wasn't sure what to expect and was confused when I read, "Sorry, try next time."

Merlin was in full flow: "Years ago, some promotional guru had this idea of turning the bottle cap into an instant-sweepstakes vehicle to increase purchases. And it worked. But now that everyone is doing it, the consumer is beginning to expect it. And if the soft drink manufacturer stops doing it, the consumer opts to buy another drink that does. It doesn't do much to build brand loyalty.

"Pepsi understood this and developed a loyalty program that provided points, just like the airlines did with frequent-flyer miles. The program keeps building loyalty through new and imaginative sweepstakes. One of my favorites provided the ultimate control by letting you create your own odds of winning! The prize was a free Xbox 360 given away every ten minutes. The process was simple—under every cap of Pepsi or Mountain Dew was a code number. You logged onto a dedicated Web site, typed in the code, and were awarded a point. The more codes you entered, the more points you received, entitling you to participate in the sweepstakes more often. You could select, up to three days out, the date and time (in increments of ten minutes) that you wanted to enter the sweepstakes. The time of day you entered determined your odds. For example, Sunday night at 7:20 might have 2,605 entries and a Monday morning at 7:20 might have 1,507. So by entering in the morning time slot you increased your chances of winning. You controlled your own odds!

"But," Merlin added, "you ain't heard nothing yet. Would you like to learn about a small business that lets you control your own price?" Without waiting for the obvious answer, he continued with a fascinating story about a small business that found a way to leverage trust and build loyal customers.

"You are probably not aware," smiled Merlin, "but you are sitting with an accomplished author of a number of books. One of my most popular is *Extreme Card Tricks: The Handbook of Cuts, Shuffles, and Forces.* I'm surprised it hasn't made it on to the *New York Times* Bestseller List. Every magician I know has read it."

I reluctantly confessed that it hadn't made it to my bookshelf.

"I too have a confession," confided Merlin. "I might be great at manipulating coins and cutting cards, but my grammar and spelling are, hoola-boola, embarrassing. I knew I had to find a service that would make me a grammar/spelling wiz. So I began my search.

"Naturally, I went to the Web, typed in 'proofreading service,' and—kowie-bumba—I was bombarded with more choices than I ever imagined. More than two million! It was overwhelming. Filtering the good services from the bad appeared more challenging than my first lesson in learning to levitate myself."

Then Merlin stood up. He walked back a couple of steps and began to rise in the air. I could not believe it. Nor could the people sitting at the table next to us. Before I could ask how he could accomplish such a feat, he lowered himself to the ground and continued talking as if nothing miraculous had just happened. "Luckily, a friend of mine told me of a service called Proofread*NOW*. It's an unbelievable service model."

"More unbelievable than what I just saw you do?" I asked, still not believing my own eyes.

"I could teach anyone to do that trick," he said. "But having a proofreading service with an editorial staff at my beck and call, as if they were in the room next door—that is a true miracle.

"The moment you go to the Web site, it's choice and control all the way. For example, my first concern was how much it would cost to use the service. I decided to comparison shop and clicked through to a few of the other offerings. Here's a quick summary of two experiences in comparative price shopping."

The word had gotten out, and Merlin had attracted a small group waiting to see him levitate again. Noticing the number of people he said, "These are all real companies but I won't use their real names to protect the innocent—you never know who is listening!

"On MakeNoMis-Steak, there is no telephone number you can call for pricing or turnaround-time information. You must send in the document and in return, you will receive a detailed cost summary. There is no obvious information regarding even the turnaround time for the quote. This required a lot of effort on my part that did nothing to build a trusting relationship.

"On ProofsinthePudding.com, an instant estimate is offered. You submit the number of words and they quickly e-mail an estimate that is quite reasonable. But to get a firm quote you must submit the document with the promise of a response somewhere between thirty minutes and twelve hours. This process first builds a relationship by offering me quick turnaround, and then goes back to square one because of all the conditions attached to getting the real quote.

"Then I visited ProofreadNOW.com. I clicked 'Prices' on the navigation bar and it clearly laid out the cost while instantly letting me know that I was calling the shots. I could pick the level of service: spelling, grammar, and clarity, or all that plus style as well. I could pick the price based on turnaround time: a one-page, five-hundred-word document costs $27 with a one-hour turnaround, $11 with a twenty-four-hour turnaround, and a range of prices in between. In fact, I could pick the exact hour I wanted the document sent back to me. I could pick the format and typeface, and specify any special requests.

"I felt like I was at Starbucks ordering a double espresso with a shot of soymilk. Except I could also control the price by specifying how fast I wanted the coffee served. Thinking about how much I wanted to spend and how quickly I needed it back was also making me part of the act. My relationship with ProofreadNOW had already begun even before I signed up.

"I had to meet this 'magician' and contacted the owner of the company," Merlin added. "It turns out he is an entrepreneur and successful software developer who happens to be a perfectionist—particularly with writing. The 'magician's' name is Phil Jamieson, and he shared with me a charming story illustrating the happenstance of creating a successful business:

> In the eighties, I was a charter subscriber to a literary magazine whose editor lacked the resources for proofing the articles. This proved a distraction for me, so I contacted the editor and offered to proofread the articles, if they were sent to me via e-mail. This was in the prehistoric times of the Internet, so I taught him how to employ change tracking and sent the proofread articles back to him. Lo and behold, the articles I worked on were showing up in the magazine. I am sure the readers appreciated this, as did the editor, who asked me to continue proofreading articles. It was a labor of love for me.
>
> During this time, my software company was heading one way and I was headed in another, looking for new opportunities. I thought, Why not take this model and have people with the time and resources to proofread help people who have neither the time nor resources? This is still the model we have today. The general assumption in the proofreading business is that writers, editors, and scholars are the typical audience in need of this service. But the response from advertising agencies, public relations firms, and ordinary businesses tell us we've hit a real need.

I definitely was going to share all these examples with my team. There must be a dozen ways of using choice and control to build and strengthen our customer relationships.

Then Merlin shouted out abruptly. "Stand up straight and when I say 'now!' hold your breath for as long as you can.

"Now!"

I took a deep breath and he began counting off the time. I never realized how long twenty seconds could be—then thirty, then fifty, and by sixty-five seconds I had turned tomato red.

"You must be a runner," he observed. "Most people don't make it past twenty-five seconds." Then he told me about Houdini's unique ability to get people to experience the magic in a trick before he even began the trick. I was about to learn of Houdini's famous milk-can escape that began when the legendary magician walked out onstage and invited the audience to hold their breath as long as they could.

"After the last person holding their breath almost fainted, Houdini would bring out a large milk can," said Merlin excitedly. "The audience would be allowed to inspect the milk can and the locks used to secure the top. Then Houdini would squish himself into the can as his assistants poured water on top of him until the brim was overflowing. The top would be secured, and then locked. A curtain was draped around the milk can, and the tension began.

"Now here's the secret to the trick," Merlin said quietly. "Houdini preengaged his audience by making them part of the act. In other words, they were already sold on the trick before the trick began."

Sensing that the concept had not totally sunk in, he continued. "Within thirty seconds of Houdini being submerged in water, there was a rustle and a little nervous laughter in the audience. People became a little uncomfortable. At forty seconds, people started to get concerned. At sixty seconds they

Harry Houdini performs the great milk-can escape. (1908. Library of Congress, *The American Variety Stage: Vaudville and Popular Entertainment, 1870–1920.*)

were alarmed. At around ninety seconds, someone would faint. At two minutes, people would start to get up, ashen. They did not know what to do. Everyone in the audience knew what it felt like to hold their breath until they almost fainted because Houdini preengaged them."

"How did the trick end?" I asked.

"He could be on his way out in sixty seconds, the length of time you held your breath just now, but the audience wouldn't know it," Merlin said, smiling. "Houdini would wait behind the curtain until the audience was at the point of pandemonium and then he would suddenly appear, exhausted and panting, as if he had just looked death in the eye." Merlin paused reflectively and then asked, "Do you recall the picture of me and the mayor that was framed in the magic shop?" Actually, I did, and told him that I was quite impressed that he was a friend of New York's mayor.

"That's some foolaboola from the Isle of Malagoola!" kidded Merlin. "I knew him; he didn't know me. If you took a picture of that picture being taken, you would have seen a hundred people in line, waiting to shake his hand. By making myself part of his act, I bring him into my office, hang him on the wall, brag about what a nice guy he is, and spread some votes."

Something didn't make sense. "Isn't a free trial or giveaway a form of preengagement?" I asked.

"No," responded Merlin. "When you give something away for free, there is no emotional commitment on behalf of the receiver. There is no choice and no control. The key to preengagement is getting the consumer to make an emotional commitment through an action they perform, versus getting something they did not ask for or seek, such as a free sample.

"Let me demonstrate," he said, as he reached into his pocket and pulled his hand out in a fist. "When I was a kid," he confided, "I used to go outside with something in my hand. My goal was to stand in the ninety-degree heat and count 'one one thousand, two one thousand, three one thousand, and four one thousand.' You know what I was doing?"

"Burning ants?" I joked.

"Never thought of doing that," he said, looking at me a little strangely. Opening his fingers, he said, "Look." I saw six

M&M's in the soft palm of his hand. "I wanted to see how long it would take before these candies would melt," he said.

"Back then, the M&M's advertising tag line was, 'The milk chocolate melts in your mouth—not in your hand.' I did not believe the advertising and wanted to see how long it would take the M&M's to melt. Kids did not have disposable income then, so the advertising was directed at the parents. In 1995, Masterfoods, the manufacturer of M&M's, adopted a new strategy that changed the future of their business. They began to focus on color, using one of the most brilliant preengagement techniques in twentieth-century marketing. They asked people to vote on the next color for M&M's."

"Purple was my vote," I blurted out.

"Good color, but wrong choice, at the time," Merlin said consolingly. "10,234,142 Americans voted. Fifty-four percent voted for blue. It's my theory that Masterfoods quickly learned a new secret—you preengage your customer by giving them choice and control."

Merlin was right. In the early nineties, consumers didn't have choice and control over the manufacturing of a product, yet Masterfoods gave me that power by allowing me to decide. I even remember having a debate with my wife on the color they should go with.

"The concept of preengagement was so powerful that M&M's repeated the voting in 2002 on an ever grander scale by asking the world, 'What color would you choose?' Your color purple showed up again, along with pink and aqua. This time you won. More than ten million people from two hundred countries in the Global Color Vote chose purple."

Then something dawned on me, and I asked Merlin if I could see one of the M&M's he was holding.

"These are different from regular M&M's," I declared. "The initials are MGM."

"Merlin George Miles," said the magician. "These are customized M&M's. There is a special Web site called the M&M's Brand Store. You can pick your colors. If you are celebrating the birth of a boy, you can pick white and blue M&M's. A girl, pink and white M&M's. You can pick your school colors. You can have them packaged in five or six different ways."

"This is terrific," I said excitedly. "My wife's birthday is coming up and she's an M&M's fanatic. She'll flip out to see her initials on her favorite colors."

"This is the power of preengagement," Merlin pointed out. "You are already pre-sold on buying them and you haven't even asked the price, which, by the way when I last checked, is $11.25 per eight-ounce bag, with a minimum order of four bags. A steep price, but one you are willing to pay for being part of the act.

"In the early nineties, the concept of selling customized clothing, like sneakers, was just that—a concept. Today, Nike lets you customize your own shoes on NIKEiD. The experience of choosing your style, fabric, and color is as thrilling as watching a tape of Slydini, one of the world's greatest sleight-of-hand magicians, lifting a coin and making it disappear within inches of your face. A significant number of all Nikes sold on the Internet are sold through this site, even though customers pay a premium for having the choice and control. The brand experience is so effective that Nike allows other shoe distributors to utilize the NIKEiD technology on their own sites.

"They also expanded the experience on digital billboards. On Forty-fourth and Broadway is the Reuters building, displaying one of the most interactive digital billboards ever created and comprised of millions of LEDs. It's the largest sign in Times Square, running twenty-three stories high, and even so can be missed among all the other competing signs. Knowing this, Reuters looks for ways of making the billboard more of an event than a display.

"R/GA, an advertising agency for the digital age, created the technology for the billboard, then added drama to the technology; first for Yahoo!, then Nike," said Merlin.

"R/GA was asked to make the sign 'dramatically' interactive. The first time was for Yahoo! in 2004, when they were relaunching their automotive section. A two-player game on the sign controlled by cell phones was developed. The Reuters Sign invited you to dial an '800' number. If you were the lucky caller, you got control of a car and could drive it using the keypad on your phone: 2 to accelerate, 8 to slow down, 4 to turn left, and 6 to turn right. The game ran for nearly two weeks during the 2004 New York Auto Show.

"When NIKEiD.com launched at the beginning of 2005," Merlin continued, "the Reuters Sign offered the ideal interactive solution. The sign could be controlled using cell phones. So it was just a matter of developing a NIKEiD version, where a shoe appeared on the screen.

"The caller who dialed at the right moment got control of the sign for sixty seconds, making color selections using the keypad on the phone. At the end of the session, the user received an SMS message on the phone with a Web address where they could pull up the shoe they had designed and purchase it."

"I always thought of 'brand' as the right message, cool logo, ad, or image," I told Merlin. "But now I am wondering if 'brand' is defined by the customer's experience prior to making the purchase as well as the actual purchase."

"Presto!" Merlin said excitedly. "You're a fast learner. Bet you'd master the Pinky Lift in no time." I later learned that this sleight of hand is an imperceptible way to separate specific cards from the deck without the participant seeing anything out of the ordinary. I did learn it, but Merlin was wrong, because I am still working on doing the move without anyone noticing it.

"But hold that thought for now," said Merlin. "We are going to discuss using experience to build the brand in another lesson."

I was so intrigued by what I had learned today that I almost forgot to share with him the outcome of the first lesson about challenging assumptions. "Merlin," I said, "you would not believe what happened a few weeks ago."

"You forget that you are talking to a magician. It's not easy to surprise me. But you have piqued my curiosity—what magic happened?"

"The group came up with a new idea: to develop our own product. Something totally unique that no one else has. Our hope is that it will provide us with more leverage with the stores than we have ever known. If we are right, customers will be clamoring for our product."

"Are you going to share your secret?" kidded Merlin.

I realized that I forgot to tell him the concept. "We are going to create a new category of salad dressings, called American dressings. The ingredients of the dressing will be indigenous to America. For example, our flagship brand will be made of New Jersey tomatoes, Virginia ham, and Wisconsin Cheddar. Our plan is to extend the line to include Boston baked beans, Florida citrus, and New Orleans Creole dressings!"

Merlin smiled and said, "It's exciting to see the outcome of deciding to look at the other hand. I love the concept. Hey, how about Idaho potato dressing? Great for picnics and mixing with scrambled eggs in the morning!"

I told him I would share it with the group.

"Please do, and while you are meeting with them, challenge them to think of ways to make the audience part of the act.

Now let's review the checklist for this lesson."

CHECKLIST FOR LESSON #2

Building Trust—
Making the Audience Part of the Act

1. Provide choice. When a magician walks into a room, everyone knows they are going to be fooled in some fashion. Distrust is a magician's occupational hazard. A magician begins building trust in the simplest way: providing a perceived freedom of choice such as selecting a card from a deck. Today's consumer requires "real" choice and the newer and greater the number of options associated with that choice, the stronger the relationship between the customer and the product or service. Starbucks began securing customer loyalty by providing innovative options: twenty ways to order your coffee, numerous places to sit—sofas, armchairs, stools, and tables—and is exploring providing MP3 "fill-ups" that transfer songs onto their customers' portable music players.

2. Offer control. Control is giving the consumer the power to influence the course of events. Pepsi created the most imaginative online sweepstakes that let you pick the number of entries, the time of entry, and, more important, the odds of winning that prize. The prize was an Xbox 360 every ten minutes. Every time you logged on you were allowed to select, up to three days out, the time you wanted to enter, in increments of ten minutes. When you entered determined your odds. For example, a Sunday night slot at 7:20 might have 2,605 entries and a Monday morning slot at 7:20 might have 1,507. So by entering in the later time slot you increased your chances of winning.

3. Generate preengagement. Houdini was a master at getting his audience to buy into the magic before the magic even began. In the beginning of his historic act, the milk-can escape, he asked the audience to hold their breath as long as they could. The seconds would be counted down until the last person let out his or her breath. Then Houdini would begin his routine of having himself locked in a milk can filled with water. A curtain was drawn around the milk can, and the time counted out. Preengaging created an emotional bond with the audience amplifying the effect of Houdini's escape. The audience knew what it was like to run out of breath, and after he spent ninety seconds in the milk can, people began to panic, faint, or leave the room.

Merlin handed me a few more M&M's and popped the rest in his mouth. "Meet me next week at the magic shop. I am going to teach you about creating a magical brand experience, and one of the ways you'll learn is by assisting me in a trick. By the way, wear some old clothes. The trick doesn't always work."

When I got back to the office, I experienced another miracle—a barrage of e-mails from my team. They wanted to know how lesson two went, and when we would be meeting again.

"Thursday at eight thirty," I e-mailed back.

The next morning I walked into the conference room ten minutes early and discovered that everyone was already there.

Buddy jumped right in. "I decided to test the idea and told a few of our distributors that we have a new kind of salad dressing. At first, everyone yawned. Then I described the ingredients in the product and how they would relate to each city and state in the country. Suddenly everyone wanted to learn more. In fact, they began to suggest ideas. Get this: Someone suggested Idaho potato dressing to pour on romaine lettuce when you're having a hamburger or steak!"

"Great idea," I said, and I smiled, thinking of Merlin's suggestion of the same thing. "It might also go with your scrambled eggs in the morning," I added.

Sunjay then told us what he had been up to. "Remember the notion I had about the differences in formula of a home-made dressing made in a kitchen processor versus a giant vat? I tracked down a food chemist and I was right. The physics of mixing large quantities is totally different. The molecules move at completely different speeds, which affects the consistency and taste. I had the food chemist sign a letter of nondisclosure and shared our idea. He loved it so much he's going to work with us at a discount to figure out how to make great-tasting big batches. He told me all he wants is his name attached to the creation of this product."

I recalled what Merlin said about how great ideas are contagious and create energy of their own.

Thelma and Deborah also had their reports on the dressing industry and discovered that bottled salad dressings are like TVs: Everyone has one or two in their house. It's a $1.7 billion industry that is growing nearly 5 percent a year.

I was proud to see the group working as a team. It was obvious Merlin's "magic" was working.

The only one who didn't seemed charged was Shawn. He

wasn't criticizing the ideas, but he wasn't contributing either. I was sure I was not the only one who was bothered by this.

"What did you learn in your last lesson?" Buddy asked me. I shared the tricks Merlin had performed, along with their lessons. We discussed how choice, combined with control, leads to trust and building long-term relationships. I explained the concept of preengagement and making the audience part of the act. It didn't take long before the ideas began flowing.

Deborah's hand shot up like she wanted to be the first to answer the teacher's question in class. "I bet there are hundreds of different types of ingredients. Why limit the recipes to our own ideas? How about if we cogenerate?"

Everyone looked at Deborah a little askance.

"What I mean," explained Deborah, "is how about we have potential customers help us develop the ideas by inviting them to suggest their own line extensions."

Atypically, Sunjay, who wasn't collaborative by nature, jumped on this idea. "I could put together a Web site that explains our concept and then allows people to suggest their ideas," he said excitedly. "While we are getting their ideas, we are also building our own database of customers. I bet if we ask them the right way, they will tell us something about themselves, kind of like qualifying them as 'real customers' down the road."

Thelma, a proponent of anything that reduced the cost of buying a list or doing focus group research, seconded the idea.

We talked about other ways to make the "audience" part of the act. Deborah suggested forming a "board of advisors" that anyone on the site could join. Their role would be to vote on the best ideas, volunteer to test different dressings, and, when the time was right, become unpaid word-of-mouth spokespeople.

We agreed to pursue these ideas as well as focus on how to

build awareness and drive people to the site. Then Chief surprised all of us with another business idea.

"I was thinking of ways we could provide choice, control, and preengagement to both the stores and customers," Chief said in an insightful manner. "As you know, one of our biggest clients orders our high-end olive oil to sell in their food-and-kitchen catalog. I went back to our sales records and discovered that they have increased their orders every year, by more than 15 percent. Thinking about what Merlin said, it struck me: Why don't we merchandise our own olive oil direct to consumers?"

I was the first to react. "But that goes against our principle of not competing with a client. Creating a new type of salad dressing is different because we don't supply that to stores."

Shawn jumped on the bandwagon of my negativity and almost screamed: "He's right. This is another example of trying to change a business model that has a history of working."

To be honest, I welcomed someone supporting me, but I didn't like the tone behind that support. I had forgotten to ask Merlin how to deal with Shawn and his resistance to new ideas. I took out a piece of paper and made myself a note to remember to ask at the next lesson.

Thelma interrupted my thought.

"Jonathan," Thelma said, in the most motherly way, "try looking at the other hand."

I was going up against three generations of thinking, but I forced myself to consider what Chief had to say. "Continue, please," I said to Chief.

"I found the story about ProofreadNOW quite compelling," he said, "which made me think of creating a customized olive oil store that was both retail- and Web-based. Customers could choose the quality of olive oil (virgin, first press, second press), the amount of olive oil (6 oz., 8 oz., 24 oz.), and the type of designer bottle it would come in (rustic, modern, tall, short, etc.). Once they purchased a bottle, they could come back to a retail store and refill it, or trade in the bottle for another. The consumer would control quality, quantity, and price. The implementation at first may be, physically, a little messy, but it's worth playing this idea out. Just as importantly, if we do it right, we will be building a very loyal, trusting customer, and potential customers for American dressings!"

The team went silent. Ten seconds later the room burst into applause, and I was clapping the hardest.

MAGIC TRICK #2

Sixth Sense

I like this trick because it can be done anywhere, without preparation. The participant has total choice and control and does all the work. The secret is in the way you count.

Effect: A participant is asked to mentally select one of six items on a dining room table. The magician points to items one at time as the participant mentally spells out the name of the item he's selected, one letter at a time. When the participant finishes spelling the word, the magician's hand is resting on the exact item.

Method: This trick can be done anywhere once you know the secret. I will use a dinner table setting as an example. The secret is to pick out six items. One that is spelled out in three letters (tea), four letters (salt), five letters (water), six letters (pepper), seven letters (flowers), and eight letters (olive oil). The first two times you point to an item, point at any item. Then point to the three-letter word, then the four-letter word, then the five-letter word, etc. When you are told to stop, your finger will be on the item that the participant mentally selected.

Performance: "Food doesn't just feed the body. It also feeds the mind, making it stronger, even telepathic. Let me demonstrate now that we've had our appetizers."

(Pick out two items that are made up of three letters each. Let's say pea and tea.) "Of these two items, which would you like me to use in my demonstration?" (Set aside whichever they select. Now select two items that are each four letters, such as fork and salt.) "Please pick one of these items." (Now select two items of five letters—plate and glass.) "Please pick one of these. Thank you. I'd like to add a few more items to make things more difficult. To speed up the process, I will pick this [six-letter item], this [a seven-letter item], and this [an eight-letter item].

"OK, we will stop here. If you'd like, you can mix the order of these items around or we can begin the magic." (Most people will want to mix the order up once or twice.)

"Excellent. We will begin by having you"—choose a participant—"think of one of the objects." Look the participant in the eye as you say, "I am going to touch an object. Each time I touch an object, you are to mentally spell out the word you are thinking of, one letter at a time. When you have spelled out the word, say 'stop!'

"Let's begin, *now!*" (Touch any of the objects). "Now for the next letter." (Touch any object). "Again." (Now touch the three-letter object.) "Again." (Now touch the

four-letter object. Continue the process until the participant tells you to stop. Finish the act by saying something
silly.) "Wow, that took more energy than I thought. I'm
glad I ordered the . . . [pick an item like steak]." Then take
your bow.

DEFINING YOUR BRAND—CREATING A MAGICAL EXPERIENCE

Over the next few weeks we explored an endless flow of possibilities that kept us so busy I almost forgot my next lesson with Merlin.

Remembering his warning, I left my office wearing an old T-shirt and paint-spattered blue jeans. I arrived at Merlin's shop just as he was showing his last customer how to take a borrowed dollar bill and make it float three feet off the ground. Before the customer could mutter, "How'd you do that?" Merlin politely pointed to the sign behind him that read: WE SHOW YOU THE SECRET—AFTER YOU PAY FOR THE TRICK. Without flinching, the customer took out his credit card and almost ran out of the store in anticipation of showing off this incredible illusion.

"Hoola-boola!" said Merlin, as if he had just noticed me entering the store. "Are you here today to learn or to patch the cracks in the ceiling?"

Before I could remind him that it was his idea to dress this way, the magician pushed a picture into my hand. It was an old, black and white photograph of a man standing underneath a giant elephant five times his size. He was posed like a conductor, both hands raised, willing the elephant to stand on her two hind legs. The photo was taken from the back of the stage, depicting the packed theater where every face in the audience stared up in amazement.

"It's not easy to recognize the man in the photo," admit-

Houdini and Jennie the elephant, performing at the Hippodrome, New York. (1918. Library of Congress, *The American Variety Stage: Vaudeville and Popular Entertainment, 1870–1920.*)

ted Merlin, "because his head is bent back and his face is up, looking into the elephant's eyes, but that's Harry Houdini. The theater where this historical event took place was called the Hippodrome, the first modern entertainment center in America, located in New York City on what is now Forty-third Street and Sixth Avenue. It opened April 12, 1905, with 5,200 seats, and enjoyed an illustrious, if short-lived, run as the largest theater in New York. Just before the Hippodrome closed in 1928, to be converted to a movie house, Harry Houdini created the greatest illusion the world had every seen. He made Jennie, a ten-thousand-pound elephant, disappear before a sold-out crowd.

"What's as fascinating as the illusion," said Merlin, "is the effect it had on the audience. Only a limited number of people actually saw the illusion happen, due to a narrow sight line between the stage and the opening in the large container Jennie had entered. Yet each and every person in the packed theater knew that he or she had just witnessed a miracle. It didn't take long for everyone in the Hippodrome to get caught up in the emotion of the experience. So while a few thousand people claimed to have seen the miracle that day, a million people had heard about it by the end of the month.

"Houdini had been searching for a way to connect himself with his audience that would go beyond great reviews and sold-out crowds. He wanted to create an experience that would immortalize him," said Merlin. "Making Jennie vanish was an experience on such a grand scale. In other words, Houdini didn't achieve fame by describing what he did; he sought out a way for each and every person to experience something new and great.

"And that's what today's lesson is all about—creating a magical experience that defines your brand. This is why Houdini, Thurston, and Blackstone are still household names today, even though they are no longer with us. These master magicians understood that the key to fame lay in building a long-lasting, emotional relationship with their audiences. In a sense, they were marketing futurists who understood that at the end of the day, it wasn't the advertising that defined the brand . . . it was the audience's experience. I think of it this way: Experience *is* the brand!

"Any business, big or small, can learn from these or other great magicians. Collectively, today's businesses pump hundreds of millions of dollars into creating brochures, print ads, television commercials, Web sites, and direct mail pieces designed to build a bond with the customer. Thousands upon thousands of hours are spent exploring imaginative ways to describe a product or service, to point out its 'unique selling proposition' with an ultimate goal of getting you to buy what is being sold. This formula worked well forty years ago when there were few competing products or services, when there were a handful of TV channels to watch or magazines to read, when the retail store was the only place in town to buy something, and when the majority of consumers believed what they read or saw.

"Today it's a different world. There are more products than purchasers, and buyers multitask on computers, cell phones, and TVs. There are a dozen different places to buy—from stores to the Internet, from a catalog to the cell phone. Today's consumers are skeptical, well informed, and overwhelmed—bombarded by more messages in a day than in the entire lifetime of someone living in the Victorian age.

"Marketers are aware of these changes, but that doesn't make adapting to them any easier. Car manufacturers still spend billions of dollars a year on TV commercials even though 70 percent of new car buyers go to the Internet first to help them decide what to buy. This has forced Detroit to seriously re-explore its marketing strategies regarding mass media."

As I digested what Merlin said, I recalled a conversation I had had with Buddy. He wanted me to approve an advertising budget for new marketing materials for American dressing—a print ad, a full-color brochure, a Web site, and a product demo video. But something about his request bothered me. I couldn't verbalize it at the time, but I knew it wasn't just the money I was approving. It was also the company's time: writing the copy, working with outside sources and resources, meeting to discuss materials, making decisions, and giving approvals. I realized that before we jumped into marketing we needed to identify ways to bond with our clients and customers that would define our marketing materials. We needed to explore the experiences that would define our brand in a way that was more powerful than any advertising we employed.

But I had no idea where to begin, and I told Merlin exactly that.

"I guess if you knew," he laughed, "you wouldn't be here. So let me give you three important guidelines to creating an experience that defines the brand: adding drama, providing discovery, and listening while performing. Let's tackle drama first."

Merlin pulled out a pack of midsize Styrofoam cups, ripped open the top, pulled out a cup, and placed it on the counter. "Do me a favor," directed the magician. "Open the bottle of water next to me."

Twisting off the cap, I handed him the bottle. He poured the water into the cup.

"You'll be glad you wore what you wore today," Merlin said reassuringly and, without asking permission, held the filled cup over my head.

"What happens next," he said, "relies on two things—my skill in making the water disappear, and my luck in actually making it happen. Sometimes neither takes place. So with your permission, I would now like to turn the cup upside down!"

Curiosity gave me no choice but to say yes.

"Uncle-barrel-feffer," shouted Merlin, as he quickly turned the mouth of the cup over my head. I flinched, expecting the worst. But nothing flowed out. Not a drop. The water was gone. I felt baffled, relieved, and wowed!

"I love this trick for two reasons," he said. "First, it's an incredible effect that you never forget. Second, it illustrates an important insight: Magic is technology with drama."

"All magic?" I asked.

"Not all, but many of the most memorable tricks are," Merlin explained. "Magicians love to twist technology into the most interesting and imaginative tricks and illusions. In 1895, a French general commissioned Jean Eugène Robert-Houdin (the father of modern magic, from whom Houdini got his name) to demonstrate France's superiority in Algeria. Performing for Arab tribes, Houdin would invite a local leader up to the stage to lift a trunk, which was done immediately and with ease. A second later, upon Houdin's command, the leader would try again, but would lose his strength and be unable to lift the trunk. Houdin was using the advanced technology of electromagnetism set up under the stage to lock down the steel trunk upon his signal.

"It's rumored that the disappearing water trick you just witnessed originated from a conversation a magician was having with his son who worked at a manufacturer of adult diapers. Apparently, the technology that allows the diaper to retain water is similar to the technology used to create the illusion of the water disappearing from the cup. But I'm going to let you figure out what that technology is. It's a good exercise in how to *follow the other hand*.

"Another trick demonstrating this principle is patent number PAT0928AA2E applied for by Joseph A. Karson in 1940," announced Merlin. "This illusion is called the 'Zombie Ball' and sixty-six years later it's still one of the most popular acts in magic. Lance Burton's first performance on Johnny Carson's *Tonight Show* in 1981 included the 'Zombie Ball,' and Burton still does a version of it today. This masterpiece has many variations in performances but originated with the magician making a solid silver shining ball float on the edge of a large silk, behind the magician's back and high into the air. Karson claimed that his inspiration came from repairing a toilet! While he was looking at the various dismantled parts his eye gravitated to the toilet float—a hollow ball and metal rod—and he wondered if there was another application for it. Using a bathroom towel he began experimenting. The rest is history, and it's been on the 'rise' ever since!"

I cringed at the pun and shot right back.

"Sounds like a lot of crap to me," I said in a way that set the challenge for the next pun.

"Before our conversation goes down the drain," replied Merlin, "watch this."

Suddenly, he reached behind my ear and pulled out what looked to be a potato chip with writing on it. "It's called a Pringles Print, and the million-dollar question is," mused Merlin, "is this a food you play with or a game you eat? Procter & Gamble turned a proprietary way of printing on a paper-thin, curvy chip into a dramatic new interactive food. Using red and blue food dye, Pringles teamed up with Trivial Pursuit and created 2,400 unique questions and answers that appear individually on these stackable chips."

Merlin popped a chip into his mouth. His message was slowly sinking in. "I suppose you could substitute the word 'innovation' for 'magic,'" I suggested.

"You're amazing. That is correct," he said, quite pleased. "Innovation is technology with drama, and it's one of the most powerful ways to create a customer experience that generates a

Wow! Think about the first time you listened to an iPod, experienced instant messaging on your computer, or used your cell phone to play a song—it felt like magic. And the companies that recognize this are the ones that are going to win.

"Everyone had access to DIRECTV, but JetBlue found a dramatic way of using it by being the first to put TV screens on the backs of all its seats. All the recording companies had information on the latest technology for downloading music, but it was Apple that created iTunes, and now it is one of the largest music stores in the world.

"Another wonderful example of how to add drama to technology is the Spin Pop lollipop marketed by one of the most successful product entrepreneurs, John Osher. This bestselling battery-powered candy has a handle that spins the lollipop around for the child to lick. Priced at an unheard of $2.99 per lollipop, more than sixty million were sold. John is brilliant at whatever he does, from inventing gadgets designed for everyday household needs to investing in hit Broadway shows like *Hairspray*. Part of his success lies in challenging assumptions. When an engineer tells him it can't be done, he knows he's on the right track, and tells the engineer to find a way to do it anyway. A few years ago, he added drama to technology to create the most successful product launch ever for Crest, one of Procter & Gamble's most famous brands.

"Osher began by choosing an effect: creating an electric toothbrush for $1 more than a manual brush. The Spin Pop had taught him how small motors work and how to produce the mechanics cheaply. Utilizing this knowledge, he and his team invested $1.5 million and eighteen months to create a $5 electric toothbrush. Procter & Gamble, which began as a marketing partner, ended up buying John's company for $475 million. The product the partnership produced? The Crest SpinBrush.

"Osher's performance challenged assumptions every step of the way. The product was launched with no advertising, and the packaging allowed the consumer to turn on the brush while in the store (many experts believed this would be a costly error that drained the battery before purchase). The SpinBrush was an instant hit, and more than 500 million of these gadgets have scrubbed the world's teeth," exclaimed Merlin.

"Why didn't the other electric toothbrush manufacturers develop this product first? After all, they were the experts at this technology," I asked

"I asked John the same question and you know what he told me?" Merlin smiled.

They were all following the wrong hand. They were going against each other saying these are the rules of electric toothbrushes. They must cost $50 to $75. They must last three years and do all this and all that. And they all use Rolls-Royce-quality motors and expensive parts, and they're basically relatively low volume–high margin. And that's where their whole focus is. Nobody, because of that, would even think that it's possible to manufacture something for $1.40.

Now I could because I've been making battery-powered candy items for 80 cents. I've 60 cents more to spend. What have I got to do? I have to waterproof it. I have to add bristles. I have to get enough torque. But otherwise, I'm using similar motors, batteries, packaging, and everything else. So I've got 60 cents to do this. My view could not have been understood by those companies. It would have never entered into their minds.

"But I am not a tech kind of guy," I confessed to Merlin. "The concept of adding drama to technology is beyond me.

I'm incapable of fixing a toaster, let alone fixing a computer or writing a software program."

"You don't even have to know how to use a cell phone to achieve *Wow!*" Merlin said. "You just need to identify these three things, and there's no specific order: a customer need, a technology, and drama."

Merlin then handed me a folded paper bag and asked me to press down hard. I did as told until my hands turned red and the bag was absolutely flattened.

"I asked you to press down," he said as he took the bag back, looking offended, "but I didn't mean that hard. I hope you didn't damage the goods."

With that, Merlin unfolded the bag, opened it up, and, looking inside, pulled out what looked like a soda bottle filled with green liquid.

"My favorite flavor: Green Apple soda. I picked it out especially for you." Merlin smiled.

He handed me the bottle. I was shocked. There was no way that bottle could have been in the bag. I remembered that his hands were empty before he took the bag back. My mind was racing with theories on how it was accomplished. Then I looked at the label and instantly stopped thinking about how the trick was done. I was now thinking about something even more amazing.

Below the bold typeface that read jones soda green apple was a picture—a picture of me!

"Don't you remember?" said Merlin. "I took that picture at Victoria's Secret. But I can see in your eyes that you are wondering how that picture got to be on the label of a soda bottle. This is a very interesting story. Grab a seat.

"The story of Jones Soda is quite remarkable, because it reflects all three key guidelines on using experience to build a brand. Back in 1987, Peter van Stolk founded a soda distribution business in western Canada. He was a natural at figuring out which soft drink flavors would sell and which wouldn't. Eight years later, he founded his own manufacturing company, later renamed Jones Soda. Peter has created an amazing company that truly knows how to bond instantly with its customers while differentiating Jones Soda from the dozens of established brands, some of which are four hundred times Jones's size.

"The company's most distinctive trademarks are their quirky flavors like Crushed Melon, Berry Lemonade, and Turkey and Gravy soda — made especially for Thanksgiving — and the labels on the bottles: pictures of people, pets, and favorite things submitted by anyone who wants to be part of the Jones Soda family.

"The first time I heard about Jones Soda was from Cardone," continued Merlin, "a successful magician, ventriloquist, and escape artist based in New York. Before he became a full-time magician, he was a bass player in a rock band. Someone in the band submitted the group's picture, and Cardone and his group ended up on the label. Friends began calling to tell him that they were seeing him everywhere. After hearing this story, I found myself going out of my way to look for Jones Soda in stores, in order to see who else made it onto the label.

"The label directs you to their Web site—which is an experience in itself. It feels more like a visit to a community of like-minded people rather than a visit to a manufacturer of sodas. You are immediately invited to submit a quote or photo for a label. Or you can vote on more than 400,000 photos that have been submitted. You can create your own customized bottle labels, which is what I did for you. You can rate or review more than twenty soda flavors or propose your own for consideration. There's a link to MyJonesMusic, where the heroes are not the manufacturers but independent musicians sharing their ideas and songs with you.

"The Web site also shares the history of the company. Peter's first step in creating the company was to choose to challenge the assumptions of a soft drink industry that focused on national distribution in the local delis and brand-name retail shopping outlets. He chose to follow the other hand and, in doing so, saw an alternative distribution strategy that placed its own coolers bearing their signature flames in some truly unique venues, such as skate, surf, and snowboarding shops, tattoo and piercing parlors, as well as in individual fashion stores and national retail clothing and music stores. Peter then expanded Jones through an up-and-down-the-street 'attack'—cold-calling and door-to-door selling—placing his product in convenience and food stores. Today, Jones Soda can be found at such places as Starbucks, Panera Bread, Barnes and Noble, Safeway, Target, Cost Plus World Market, Meijer, Winn-Dixie, Albertsons, and 7-Eleven stores.

"My instinct told me that none of this would have happened if Jones Soda had not personalized the labels—a true bonding experience. I had to find the guy and give him a call. I connected with Peter and discovered that he isn't the typical CEO and is very much like his product—a bit quirky, funny, full of energy, and with a voice that sounds like eternal youth. His cadence reminds me of a skateboarder from the seventies. But what he has to say is as sharp and poignant as any CEO on the fiftieth floor.

> Merlin, what happens in business, and this is my opinion, is that most companies typically look at their competitors from the perspective of "what are they doing?" and then they follow them. Well, end result: You're not going to be successful. You have to do it your way, and it is harder, scarier. It's a bit more challenging, but that's what I believe. Because when you get known for doing what

you do, you instantly become a leader in the category, and people respect you in a different way and they buy you. That's really important when you're creating a brand, because for beverage companies, there are many great brands.

The world has enough soda, you know what I mean? We had to make our brand relevant and meaningful to someone. We could come up with a name, we could come up with a design, but really is that relevant to somebody? What becomes relevant is when you can put your daughter on the bottle or you can put your loved ones on the bottle or you can send
any photo that you've taken and that ends up on the bottle.

"According to Peter," said Merlin, "when he decided to personalize the labels, the technology did not exist. And because it didn't exist, no one understood the value in doing it.

I remember when we talked to our label manufacturer and bottlers. They just gave us a look like "why are you doing this?" "No one does this," they said. So in the end, we just did it.

It wasn't easy. A whole bunch of work went into it and a lot of thought. But it's like anything. You first try it, you try it again, and you try it again, and ten years later it's working pretty well. Initially, we could only do small, personalized runs. But today we can do one bottle, a hundred bottles, a thousand bottles, ten thousand bottles, a hundred thousand bottles.

Merlin wondered why other companies hadn't picked up on Jones Soda's concept of personalized labels on bottles and posed the question to Peter.

Because we have the patent on it. That's one of the things
that you have in this business, you have the ability to protect
your intellectual property, and we've certainly done that.

"In essence," Merlin told me, "adding drama to technology
can start at any point. You can identify a need first. Jones Soda
began by looking for an element of drama that allowed them to
be more than just another soda. They used the technology of
printing to create personalized labels. This addressed a need
on behalf of their customers, which we will discuss next.

"The lesson within this lesson is that you can proceed from
any point within the cycle in adding drama to technology."

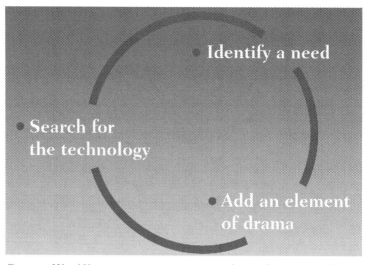

Creating *Wow!* You can start at any point in the circle to create *Wow!*
Just make sure you address all three elements.

Merlin paused. "I have often wondered what elevates a
good magician to a great one. After all, a magician today has
access to almost any magic trick. In fact, many magicians
perform exactly the same tricks. I talked to some of my fellow

colleagues about this and learned an interesting story about one of the most successful entertainers in the world: David Copperfield. He makes more money than Madonna, more than Elton John. Some believe he's successful because he does what no one else has done, like making the Statue of Liberty disappear.

"I believe his success is the process he employs to connect with his audience. He didn't just become famous overnight. He made a conscious decision early on in his career: to go to his audience, rather than wait for it to come to him. David performs on the road more than any other magician of his era. Even with his success today, he gives four hundred performances a year, often traveling to countries that other magicians feel are too unimportant to visit. David's secret is giving his audience the opportunity to discover him. He becomes 'their David,' and if you visit his Web site, you'll see by the e-mails sent to him how dedicated his audience truly is.

"Interestingly enough," said Merlin, "Peter van Stolk shared with me a similar story about connecting with his customers.

> I think that one of the big differences between Jones and a lot of other brands, and this is my opinion so it could be wrong, is that kids find it themselves. It has an emotional connection to them because they sort of discover it. It's not their parents' soda. It's their soda. They discover it; they probably spied it before someone else did.

"And that's the cool thing about Jones. They let discovery happen in multiple ways. There's a quote submitted by a customer under the cap of Jones Soda that people find relevant," shared Merlin. "There is a photo on the label. There's a Web site where you can make your own sodas. There's so much stuff going on that's relevant to you, Jones Soda becomes a totally unique experience.

"And this experience," said Merlin, "has a direct effect on advertising—they need very little of it. Peter told me:

> Our advertising budget last year was just under $800,000 on whatever it was we sold, $28 million and change. So I think that's about 3.5 percent or 4 percent. Math is not really my forte.
>
> Advertising doesn't create the brand. In a world where the average North American consumer sees three thousand marketing messages a day, you just can't buy that much space. I think what you're seeing now is that brands have to be relevant to everything and be relevant to consumers, and relevancy is what I believe. Creating that emotion is part of the relevancy process. If it's just a product, you're not going to be relevant.
>
> I think the most interesting thing is that we don't advertise the fact that people send their photos in. The only advertising that you see for it is contained in photos on the side of the Jones label, saying send us your photos. If we like them we'll put them on the label. So, one of the things I've made a really conscious effort to do is not to advertise that send-us-your-photo program. Everything has got to be discovered. Discovery is an experience.

I thought about what Merlin and Peter were saying, and it became apparent that creating a brand begins with the purchaser's experience with that brand, not the advertising and marketing around the brand. If I wanted any of our new businesses—the creation of American dressing or our custom-ized olive oil business—to succeed, we had to first consider ways to add drama to create *Wow!* and to find innovative ways to let our customers discover who we are in a relevant way. I was anxious to get back to the group and begin discussion, but Merlin told me he had one more point to cover.

"Listening while performing leads to creating great customer experiences," he confided. "A magician knows how he is doing in real time, if he listens. This is one of the most crucial talents of any magician.

"Cardone, who I mentioned before as being on the Jones Soda label, calls it 'creative intelligence'—having the ability to respond to the moment by listening to your audience. Sometimes the message is obvious. Don't pick someone from the audience to assist you if their arms are crossed or they refuse to look you in the eye. Watch for those who choose to sit in the front row or smile during the performance; they are potential participants.

"Jeff McBride, a master teacher and world-famous magician, loves to tell a story about a particular mishap," chuckled Merlin.

"Jeff has performed around the world for kings, queens, presidents, and hundreds of thousands of other people. His act is incredibly diverse—from magically transforming himself into mythical characters using ancient masks to producing rivers of coins from an unsuspecting child's nose, ears, belly button, backside, etc. He's a true professional who shows up at any performance venue two hours in advance and often changes the seating in the room if the floor plan is not conducive to his performance. Yet even with all this planning, the unexpected can happen. Jeff told me this story:

> *I was performing for a group of three hundred school-children and doing one of my regular acts—pulling forty-five feet of multicolored paper from my mouth. The kids were in awe, until I finished and inadvertently handed the*

birthday boy the mound of paper with the last part that had just come out of my mouth. This was the one section that had become slightly wet, sitting in my mouth the longest.

"Ahh . . . gross!" three hundred children cried out in unison. I probably had another thirty minutes left in the show. But at that point, the act was over.

But this led to a whole new act. My audience was telling me something, which made me consider what I needed to do to avoid this disaster from ever happening again. My solution was to take a large magic wand and through my own "hocus-pocus" secure the end of the last mound of multicolored paper to the end of the wand.

Now when I finish pulling the last of the paper from my mouth, I magically attach it to the large wand, hand it to the boy or girl, and have him or her walk down the aisle. What a sight. . . . the child walking by himself, all eyes staring, holding a wand, trailing this incredible lead of colored paper. Your audience can be your best instructor.

Merlin laughed as he told me Jeff McBride's story. "You know, many magicians don't learn from their acts. They think they are smarter than their audience. If an audience doesn't respond to their act, they try wearing flashier clothing, talking louder, or getting a prettier assistant. I have even seen magicians insult the audience for not responding in the way the magician wanted them to respond. It's just like a company whose sales are down. Instead of changing their core product or service, they change the advertising, or the advertising agency. Since I consider Peter van Stolk to also be a kind of magician, I asked how Jones Soda listens while performing.

One of the nice things about Jones, and I truly believe it, is that we're not that smart. So by taking the assumption that

*we're not that smart we have to keep it fairly simple. And
by keeping it simple we let our consumers tell us what we're
doing right and what we're doing wrong. If you really think
about the brand, Jones, it's got flavors that are submitted by
consumers, it's got labels that have their names and pictures
on them, and it has quotes under the cap that they sent us.
So you know I don't have to be that great a marketer when
everyone's sending us great stuff, you know what I mean?*

*We have a taste panel. We use kids, and part of what we
use as criteria are the categories "yummier" and "yuckier,"
or if they're older, "tastes good" or "tastes like shit." And they
tell us what they like during the conversation, and if it tastes
yummy it's good, if it tastes yucky it's on to the next flavor.*

"See how simple Peter keeps it?" Merlin pointed out. "John
Osher said the same thing. He feels it's very easy to hear what
you want if you're seeking confirmation but not the truth. He
used research on a package design as an example.

*The truth always comes out with the consumer. And some
truths are very simple. You'll show a package and it's real
pretty and you'll notice everyone likes how pretty it is.
But if you take two seconds to ask them what it says you
realize they couldn't read it. Your fonts are not right or the
contrast isn't good—simple things that could make the giant
difference between success and failure.*

Merlin stopped for a second as if something just popped
into his mind. "Jonathan, there's another person I should talk to
you about. She's a giant of a magician, though she stands only
4 foot 10. Her name is Maxine Clark, founder of Build-a-Bear
Workshop. It's one of the most successful retail operations
in this country—pure magic. Her publicly traded business

produces more than $600 of sales per square foot. Build-a-Bear is a retail experience that allows children, grandparents, parents, anyone to make their own stuffed animal. The store provides you with dozens of unstuffed bears, bunnies, and even Sesame Street characters. Pick out the one you want, then go to a stuffing station, which looks like a giant glass-enclosed machine with cotton candy flying around, and have your animal filled with soft stuffing.

"By the way, these machines already existed in China. Maxine just brought them into the retail store. Another example of adding drama to technology."

Merlin continued, "You can even put a heart and a digital chip with your own twelve-second-long recording into your animal. Once it's stuffed, it's then stitched, and off you go to a fluffing station. You then pick out an outfit—from dresses to football uniforms. The first Build-a-Bear store opened in 1997, and within eight years sold thirty-two million bears and an equal number of smiles.

"I remember," said Merlin, "asking Maxine about a rumor I had heard that she doesn't really sleep. She's told me that that's true. She gets four, maybe five hours of slumber a night. She uses a lot of her time burning the midnight oil to answer e-mails, including more than two hundred per day from kids who write to Build-a-Bear. Maxine looks at these e-mails as 'real-life focus groups,' providing insights, stories, and product suggestions that help make the Build-a-Bear experience unforgettable. And increasing profit is just one of the rewards.

"I will talk more about Maxine and Build-a-Bear in the next lesson," Merlin informed me, "but I just recalled a story she told me about how listening to your customers changes your business. She talked about how responding to one of those e-mails expanded the business.

*I don't go to bed before they're all done. They're all
personally written. So they take time and thought and, you
know, it's a part of my life. I don't handle all of them, but I
direct a lot of them to where they get handled.*

*If they're asking us for a store in Butte, Montana, I
say thank you for the suggestion on the store in Butte,
Montana. I'll forward it to our real estate department for
follow-up. Based on a number of these requests we then
discuss the feasibility of opening in Butte, Montana.*

*Many, many stores have been opened because
kids suggested them to us. I was just at an opening in
Dartmouth, Nova Scotia. A little girl, Chelsey, had written
me a long story about why we should have a store there. She
knew that we would be big at a mall. We already had had
several requests (from kids nearby), but her impassioned
plea inspired us—and we started working on the store, and
we just opened it two weeks ago. And I went there and she
came to the opening and we had a great time.*

"No type of advertising can ever produce this kind of bonding and brand loyalty," said Merlin. "There are a lot of things
we can learn from our customers, if we keep an open mind."

I remembered the term, "cogenerate," which Deborah had
used regarding engaging and listening to customers, and shared
it with Merlin.

"I like that term," he said. "It symbolizes both our need to
listen and the growing dependency on our customers for more
than just sales—as trusted allies in building our businesses."

"There is also another very important person to listen to
besides your customer," added Merlin. "Want to guess who
that is?"

"Your investors? The press? Your employees?" I offered.

"All of the above, but you left out one obvious and very influential source. Follow your other hand," said Merlin.

I thought for a moment and tried to picture who I was leaving out. Then it hit me. "Myself," I said.

"John Osher made this very apparent when he told me of a meeting he had with a bunch of experts reviewing the most recent design of the future SpinBrush," Merlin said.

We were on a conference call reviewing a prototype that had the bristles going up and down while the other one turned. We had twenty-seven people on the call, and they're reading the results of the consumer test. They're going through numbers and charts and all this crap. And I said, "Well, wait a minute, I don't get it. What did you guys think of the product? I mean, you know, sure we'll read what they all said in these tests and everything, but we've got twenty-seven people here. What'd you guys think of it?" Not one of the people had tried it.

Not one. I had, and I could sit and make comments, but not one of them had tried it. They were all willing to just listen to something they read on a piece of paper from a test. They were so unconnected. That never happened again. Every product we did after that everybody on the call had tried it and they had their own personal input.

Merlin looked at me, and then shouted, "Have you been listening to what I've been saying?"

"Absolutely," I responded, but then explained, "I was wondering how I was going to present all this to my team."

"Ah," he smiled, "I see it's time to recap the guidelines."

CHECKLIST FOR LESSON #3

Defining Your Brand—
Creating a Magical Experience

1. Create *Wow!* Innovation is technology with drama. Jones Soda found a meaningful and relevant way to make itself different from every other soft drink manufacturer; it asked people to send in photos that then appeared on labels of Jones Soda. Another example is Build-a-Bear Workshop, one of the most successful retailers in the country. Build-a-Bear Workshop took existing technology for making a stuffed bear and turned it into a retail store experience, allowing children to make their own stuffed animal.

2. Discover. Let your customers own the brand. Jones Soda spends less than $1 million in advertising dollars to produce more than $28 million in annual sales. Their secret is allowing their customers to discover the brand by putting the soft drinks in less conventional locations, using the personalized label to drive people to their Web site, and providing unique communities, such as MyJonesMusic, which supports the brand message through the experience of discovering new musical artists.

3. Listen while performing. Listen to your customers and they will tell you what they don't like, as well as what they do. Turn that feedback into new customer experiences and you've got a unique brand. Pringles Prints does this on their Web site. Pringles began printing Trivial Pursuit questions and answers on their chips. Then they invited visitors to the Pringles Prints Web site to submit new ideas for the next Pringles Prints. All ideas submitted are shared with other visitors who then rank and vote on the ideas. Pringles gets new ideas, and customers recognize that they are being listened to by the company. Everyone wins. Maxine Clark, founder of Build-a-Bear Workshop, answers more than two hundred e-mails from children every day. According to Maxine Clark, children are her most important customers and are full of wonderful ideas and ways to improve the Build-a-Bear experience. E-mails from children have helped Build-a-Bear identify where to open new stores, what new stuffed animals to carry, and what kind of clothes they'd like their bears to wear.

As I took notes I saw my reminder to talk to Merlin about Shawn. I asked what I was supposed to do with someone who is always negative and tries to squash ideas before they even are out of the box.

"Excellent question," beamed Merlin. "In our next lesson we will go to church to find the answer." He handed me a piece of paper with an address on it. "Look for the only building on the block with a steeple. I will see you there next Monday at 8:00 p.m."

Leaving him, I tried not to dwell on the significance of the location for our next lesson. Instead, I called my office on my cell phone to set up a meeting a.s.a.p. I didn't want the group putting any more energy into the marketing of our new products until we had identified the customer experiences that would add magic to our brand. Within ten minutes, I got a call back confirming a team meeting at 2:00 p.m. the next day.

That next afternoon, I presented to the group the guidelines that Merlin had provided, related the various business case histories, and invited everyone to submit their own ideas over the next couple of days.

But the group surprised me by proposing that we begin immediately. I guess they had been feeling the need to address this issue, but were unable to verbalize it. Once Merlin's lesson was put into words, ideas began to formulate. We agreed to work together over the next couple of hours. We agreed that the American dressing line would be more than a food product; it would be a community of like-minded people who are bonded by fun, adventure in eating, and a pride in where they live and the country they live in.

This opened the door to a lot of unexpected new thinking. Here are some of the ideas.

ADDING DRAMA TO TECHNOLOGY

Surprisingly, Thelma was the first out of the box.

"I got this proposal on my desk," she said abruptly, "from this plastic company that claims to make different shaped bottles on demand. They said the cost was cheap."

The team waited for her to continue.

"Maybe we make different shapes to sell in each city, like the Statue of Liberty, the Seattle Space Needle, and the Sears Tower. That would be different."

"And fun," added Sunjay enthusiastically. "We can even let the customer suggest a shape and have other customers create a recipe to fit the bottle!"

Everyone voted this a winning idea. Except for—you guessed—Shawn.

Then Deborah spoke: "I made a list of ways that we can personalize our labels. I propose we use pictures of the people who suggest the best ideas for ingredients for our dressing."

"Speaking of personalization," said Buddy, "let's invite people to write songs with an American theme—like what makes a great American."

The group thought it was a little corny until Sunjay added, "Inviting people to post their songs is hot. I can design a site allowing us to post the songs in a format that people could download to their iPods. These tunes could also accompany great recipes that use our salad dressing or our gourmet olive oils and post them as podcasts that people could download to their iPods as well. Imagine wearing your iPod to play the instructions as you cook!"

"Have you thought this out?" asked Shawn in an ice-water voice. "Those long wires on the headsets are going to get in the way of the cooking. You might even cut into one when you're looking down chopping the vegetables, or set your head on fire over the stove."

Once again Shawn was injecting his negativity, but that didn't seem to affect Chief.

"Hey, maybe Apple would like a crack at designing a headset you could wear while cooking. Let's get them involved. I'll send them an e-mail."

DISCOVERY

"As you know," I told the group next, "I've got this summer place in the North Fork of Long Island. It's in a little town called Orient, or as I like to say, the last stop before Europe.

I've got to drive through a lot of towns to get to Orient, and I've been noticing a growing number of farm stands that are popping up along the country roads. One called Latham's was even featured on the front cover of Martha Stewart's magazine.

"A lot of these stands are selling jellies, oils, and vinegars made by local farmers. I suggest we offer to put in mini-refrigerators that sell our dressing. We could even create a North Fork American dressing that uses the local produce."

Buddy cut in: "Like Long Island potatoes?"

"Cool idea," said Sunjay.

"How many people ever heard of Long Island potatoes?" asked Shawn snidely.

"Everyone on Long Island and the surrounding areas," said Deborah. "In fact, my grandfather used to own a potato farm on Long Island. They are famous in many places."

Thelma then suggested: "To keep our costs down, we could test a few bottles of Long Island potato dressing on the North Fork. See if it flies!"

"Cool," Sunjay repeated. "None of the big salad dressing manufacturers are doing this. . . . So it's our opportunity to be discovered."

Chief then added: "You'd expect women to be the main purchasers of salad dressing. But perhaps we can build up demand from men and work out a deal with auto parts dealers and car companies. We can place our product in their waiting rooms with marketing material that stresses the 'American' theme and taps into the 'made in America' theme. We could put in displays at auto body shops that feature American-made products."

Buddy looked at Chief in a strange way and said: "Salad dressing in auto stores is a bit of a stretch, Chief."

Chief smiled and said he was just following the other hand.

"I think it's a brilliant idea," said Deborah.

Everyone looked at her. Even Chief.

"When you said auto store, it made me think of my brother who loves cars and travels all over the country to see races. That made me think that a perfect venue to sell American dressing would be a NASCAR event. It's a perfect match."

A round of applause broke out, which took the energy level up a notch, kicking off another round of ideas.

Thelma thought we should approach the states themselves. State governments often promote their local produce (like New Jersey tomatoes or California cucumbers) and might be interested in displaying the dressing at their promotional events.

My son played soccer with a kid whose father worked for the marketing department of New York City. I suggested we create a Manhattan Island dressing and get the city to promote a contest asking the residents to come up with an appropriate recipe, which would be judged by the best chefs in the city. This would be a new way for a whole city to create its "own" dressing.

LISTENING WHILE PERFORMING

This was the hardest area to address since we didn't have an actual dressing yet. It also presented the greatest opportunity because we could build in ways to listen as we grew.

"I'd like to propose," said Chief, "that we sponsor a 'Made in America' Web log to sense people's attitudes toward products made in the U.S. and test our idea of an American Dressing community."

Thelma, who was one of those people who knew every state

bird, piped up. "Let's put pictures of state birds, capitals, or flags on the undersides of the bottle caps. Consumers could then redeem these for trips to various places in the country."

Sunjay then added, "This would give us a sense of who buys our products and allow us to open a dialogue with them." He gave Thelma a high five. She returned it with such force that you could see his hand turn red.

Remembering Maxine Clark of Build-a-Bear, I joked that we should all be trained to sleep less so that we made sure every e-mail sent in got responded to personally by someone close to the brand.

The ideas were flying, and we finally broke at seven that night. Deborah, who loved making lists, agreed to pull together all the ideas, sort them, and distribute copies by the next afternoon.

This was one list I was truly looking forward to getting.

MAGIC TRICK #3

Wireless Wonder

Using the technology of the cell phone makes this simple trick incredibly dramatic.

Effect: A participant chooses a card from the deck, puts the card back in the deck, shuffles it, and places all the cards back in the card pack. A magician borrows a cell phone from the audience, turns on the screen, and the picture of the selected card appears on the screen.

Method: Prior to performing, select any card from the deck and take a picture of it with your cell phone. I prefer a card like the queen of spades or king of diamonds, as they are more visually interesting than a number card.

Store the picture as your screen saver or in the picture library of your cell phone or PDA. Before you begin the effect, give your phone to someone and have them act as if it is theirs. Now you will force your participant to select the matching card using this simple crisscrossed method. Place the card you want to force on the top of the deck.

Shuffle the deck so that the card remains on top. (This is easy with a little practice.) Ask the participant to cut the deck in half by lifting off about half the pack and placing those cards down on the table. Immediately pick up the bottom half of the deck and place it across the top half, explaining that you will mark the cut. The two halves are now crisscrossed. Note: The arrow points to the original card you placed on the top of the deck before you began the trick.

Now ask to borrow a cell phone, and take the one offered by your secret accomplice. After they hand it to you, point to the deck and ask them to take the top card from the bottom half of the deck. Believe it or not, 99 percent of the participants will not realize it is the original top card. This is particularly due to the principle of time misdirection. That's it. You are all set to go.

Performance: "I'd like to show you a way to talk on a cell phone that will not cost you any money. I do it all the time, though most people don't believe me, including my [wife, boyfriend, mother… just fill in the blank]. I can tell by the look in your eye that you don't believe me either. That's why I'd like your help to prove my point.

"Please cut about half the cards off the top of the deck and place them over here." (Point to a spot next to the bottom half.) "Excellent. I will now mark the spot where you cut them." (Take the bottom half and place it criss-cross on the top half.)

"Does someone have a cell phone I can borrow? Thanks." (Then make a comment about the model of the cell phone.) "Now please take the top card from the bottom half of the deck and look at it. Place the card back in the deck, give it a good shuffle, and when you are satisfied that the deck is mixed, place it back on the table.

"Let's show everyone here that you can talk on the cell phone without being charged. All you have to do is think of what you want to say . . . in this case, think of the card you selected. I will hold up my left hand as kind of a wireless tower and it will receive your thoughts." (Hold your hand up.) "Ready? Please think hard. I am getting your signal, but it is weak. Think harder. That's not hard enough. I have to move to a different location." (Pause.) "I got it. Please take the phone and open it up." (The participant will see their card.) "Let everyone else see. That's your card, right?

But do me a favor. Let's keep this a secret. I don't want the phone company to catch on or they will find a way to charge us for this as well."

A few pointers: Don't forget to give the phone back to the person you "borrowed" it from. As a variation, if you get the participant's phone or text number you can send the file of the card selected ahead of time to his phone. Watch his face when you ask him to download the image from his own phone after selecting the card.

IDEA HECKLING—
REMOVING THE
OBSTACLES
TO THINKING
DIFFERENTLY

I took the subway to Times Square. It was Monday, the day that the Broadway theaters are "dark." But that didn't bother the thousands of people filling the sidewalks. I felt a bustling energy and an excitement from the crowd, electricity matched by the brightness of the hundreds of giant video screens and digital displays screaming for my attention. These amazing technologies made me reflect on my last lesson, and I began to imagine how I would use them in dramatic ways to promote some of our new business concepts.

I was so preoccupied playing around with different ideas that I passed Forty-sixth Street. Backtracking, I made a right turn, walked past Eighth and Ninth Avenues, and discovered the place Merlin had instructed me to find—an old church squeezed between two three-story brownstones. It was close to eight o'clock, and the people milling outside began to enter the church. There were businessmen in suits, kids with their parents, and out-of-towners looking both friendly and simultaneously apprehensive.

Another large group of people in their late twenties and thirties were hanging out outside, exchanging handshakes and hugs. Some were dressed in jeans, others sported leather motorcycle jackets. Some had shaved heads, others were covered in tattoos on their hands and arms. Some were dressed entirely in black, and others, more conventionally dressed, looked like out-of-towners, but with a difference.

For one thing, a disproportionate number of these people were tossing coins in the air, shuffling playing cards, and speaking in a language unfamiliar to me—using terms like "Elmsley Counts" and "Zarrow Shuffles."

I would later discover that they were all magicians, gathering together to watch their peers perform, as well as to honor the most famous "street" magician of all time—Jeff Sheridan. I also discovered that instead of a sermon in this church, I was going to be treated to a night of magic. This was a weekly event at the Theatre at St. Clement's Church called Monday Night Magic. There is a different show every week and this one was about to begin.

I looked for Merlin, but he was nowhere to be seen. Taking a guess, I went to the box office, gave them my name, and picked up a ticket, which seated me front row, dead center. The theater was small, with fewer than two hundred seats. The stage had a shiny black floor, with grayish curtains that served as the backdrop. Blood-red curtains hung at each side of the stage. Nothing inside looked the least bit like a church.

Sitting down, I introduced myself to a couple from Toronto who knew one of the magicians performing. On my other side was the CEO of a large, publicly traded company and his wife. They both loved magic. The lights went down and I quickly scanned the audience for Merlin—he was still nowhere in sight.

The master of ceremonies for the night's performance was Todd Robbins, a multitalented performer. He is a sideshow performer, magician, jazz pianist, and actor. The people next to me told me they had seen Todd eat lightbulbs. That night I would see him swallow three different types of swords.

Two great magicians, David Acer from Canada and the legendary Jeff Sheridan, performed for the next hour. As amazing as their acts were, I was distracted, wondering what lesson this was leading to. The answer was announced shortly.

"Ladies and germs," said Todd Robbins (apparently he and Merlin went to the same school of comedy). "This next performer needs no introduction. Every magician in the audience tonight knows him, has studied magic with him, or bought their tricks from him. For those who do not partake in the art of prestidigitation, I can only tell you that you are in for a real treat. I give you...Merlin."

The audience began to applaud as Merlin walked out onstage. The one hair wrapped around his bald head was actually combed. His normally stained shirt was pressed, clean, and bright white. His striped tie was neatly knotted. Even his pants were ironed. Unfortunately for Merlin, his fly was in the same position as when I first met him weeks before—halfway down.

I couldn't help myself. As soon as he caught my eye I placed my hand on my fly and moved it up and down as discreetly as possible. Besides, who could see? I was dead center in the front row. Merlin read my signal, promptly turned around, and turned back with his fly in the upright position. But the result was worse; part of the shirt, which was so rarely tucked in, got caught up in the fly and was now sticking out.

I cringed. The audience broke up in laughter, and I too had to admit it was a funny sight. The couple next to me gave me an approving nudge as they had watched how I signaled Merlin—I realized they thought I was part of the act.

He began with the Linking Rings. He showed three shiny metal rings, each a foot in diameter. First he demonstrated that all the rings were solid, twirling them around in his hand and clanging them together. All eyes were on him, watching his every move as he took two of the rings, gently touched them together, and suddenly connected them. He repeated this action with the third ring, which then melted onto the other two rings. Then he blew on the rings, and they instantly became unlinked. His moves were smooth and the audience was astonished at how he accomplished this magic.

Next he brought six people onstage. Everyone was given a razor blade, and Merlin directed each one to carefully cut a newspaper to demonstrate the blades' sharpness. He then got each person to state how sharp he or she thought the blades were. It became a little repetitive and I started to feel annoyed. Other than that, everything went fine until he turned to the last of the stage volunteers. This guy must have weighed three hundred pounds, was dressed in two mismatched halves of a business suit, and was swaying while standing—he looked like he had had a little too much to drink.

Slurring his words, this spectator said, "I know how thish trick ish done. My uncle ushed to do it. Let me sheeh all the bladesh and I'll show you." He began to approach the other spectators, holding out his hand in quest of the blades.

Every eye was on Merlin. The situation was out of control, and people were not only embarrassed but also concerned because of the razor blades. Merlin just smiled and walked over to the drunk.

"What is your name?" he asked.

"Robert," replied the businessman.

"Well, Robert. Here's what I suggest," Merlin said in a smooth and understanding voice. "Let me finish doing the trick. Everyone in the audience will be impressed, and they will want to know how it's done. You can then sell the secret to anyone out there."

Merlin pointed to the audience and everyone seemed to nod their head. Someone even called out, "See me after the show. I'll take two."

Merlin took the obnoxious spectator ever so gently by the elbow and walked him back to his seat. Then he whispered just loud enough for the audience to hear, "And Robert, don't forget to ask for a good price."

Everyone applauded. Robert sat down and Merlin continued performing. He swallowed the blades and the thread and pulled them out tied together. He then went into a sequence of amazing tricks, and after forty minutes of pure entertainment, he ended by making a thousand snowflakes flow from his hand.

I sat through another act before I left the show, but what amazed me was the way the audience reacted to Merlin. On my way out of the theater, I listened to everyone's comments.

They felt honored to have seen Jeff Sheridan and his masterful performance. They talked about how funny Dave Acer was and how amazing his coin and card tricks were. When they mentioned Merlin, the tone of their conversation changed and they spoke with a kind of respect and endearment. The way he treated the obnoxious drunk had created an amazing bond with the audience. I think he could have stopped performing immediately after the incident and they would have felt the same.

After the performance, Merlin came out from backstage and whisked me off to a local coffee shop.

"Your treat," he told me as he ordered a bacon burger with fries and, as an afterthought, a Diet Coke. While waiting for the food to arrive he asked me to give him my impressions of the act. I recapped what I thought about each magician.

"You describe what they did very well. But you have not

described their real magic. Never mind, we'll talk about that in our next lesson."

"It was unfortunate about the drunk," I said sympathetically.

"Ah," said Merlin. "I picked him especially for you."

"I don't understand," I said. "Why would you select someone who would intentionally ruin your act? Besides, how did you know he would be the one to do that?"

"I will answer your last question first." Merlin smiled. "It's called 'cold reading.' As we discussed in our last lesson, part of the skill involved in magic is listening to your audience. You look into their eyes, watch how they hold their hands over their chest, see if they are sitting in the front row or choose to hide themselves in the back of the theater. You see if they appear happy, see if they are talkative. I often scope out the audience ahead of time for practical purposes as well; once, a fellow magician called up a young spectator to participate in a trick that required using both hands. The magician discovered upon the volunteer's arrival onstage that her hand had a deformity, but it would have been cruel to have her sit down—he had to deal with it.

"The guy I selected tonight came into the theater, barreled down the aisle, and pushed people aside to get to his seat. I knew he'd be trouble."

"Then why pick him?" I asked. "And why for me?"

"You've mentioned that Shawn was giving you trouble, finding reasons why your team's ideas were not going to work. There is always going to be a Shawn, someone who will act as an 'idea heckler' by being uncooperative and disrupting the flow of the process. The resistance can come from anyone: a business partner, the CEO, an account executive, the sales team, vendors, or even your spouse.

"Anyone at any time can morph into an 'idea heckler' by holding on to their assumptions and scoff when you challenge them, especially if your ideas are more innovative or creative than theirs," he continued. "This behavior goes beyond dismissing good ideas. It also disrupts the flow of energy in exploring new ideas and solutions—just as the drunken businessman disrupted the flow and positive energy that the audience was feeling during my performance."

"So what is the method for handling these idea hecklers?" I asked.

"There are different schools of thought on handling hecklers," confided Merlin. "Some magicians believe that you match wits with wits, and hopefully end up the winner. Others pride themselves on developing an inventory of quick remarks or comebacks. A third school of magicians thrive on the spontaneity of their responses. The problem in this type of thinking is that you always have to win. As soon as the heckler gets the upper hand, your act is over.

"In essence, when you go one-on-one with a heckler you are entering a battlefield. This results in one person winning and the other losing. Few people have the skill to come back 100 percent of the time with clever lines that put the heckler in his place. So, like any war, there's no guarantee of the outcome."

"What do you do?" I asked.

"You have to understand the motives of the heckler," Merlin continued. "That person may be doing it for a number of reasons. They might be looking to upstage you, they might be so drunk they've lost all sense of propriety, or perhaps they are angry at the world. Most often they want the attention on them. We'll discuss these reasons in more detail later."

Merlin suddenly became very stern as he stated, "Regardless of the reasons, hecklers are disruptive and threaten your control. You cannot let them do this."

Softening his tone, he continued, "As I said, there are many ways of responding. Over the years, I've observed four general categories:

1. **Invite.** Invite the heckler onstage and make him part of the act.
2. **Insult.** Gain dominance by coming up with a clever remark that puts the heckler in his place.
3. **Imitate.** Repeat what a heckler says out loud for the audience to hear.
4. **Intimidate.** Create an atmosphere of superiority by leveraging your knowledge or skill.

"Intimidation used to be an advertising industry favorite," Merlin continued. "I have worked with people in advertising, and many of them believe that you sell ideas to clients through intimidation—you act as if you hold the secret that will sell the client's product. 'Only the Great Swami knows' is their attitude. This was a tack a lot of advertising agencies used for a period of time. However, I believe that intimidation has become an outdated mode of selling an idea. The world has become too complicated, and anyone claiming to know all the answers is inviting suspicion as to their credibility."

"What about the other approaches magicians use?" I probed.

"Sometimes these approaches work. Often they don't. But I'd like to change the focus of your question by challenging you to seek a very different solution."

Holding up his left hand, Merlin continued, "Assume the heckler is the problem. If you were to challenge that assumption and follow the other hand, what might you see?"

I didn't have to think long, as the solution seemed pretty clear. "I am the problem," I replied.

"You're getting pretty good at this," he beamed. "In magic, most heckling comes about because of a problem with the magician and his act. When you are boring, you invite heckling. When you are not connecting with or engaging the audience, you allow the heckler to seize the opportunity to disrupt your act. When you are unprepared, hecklers will gladly remind you by putting down your performance. When you pretend to be what you are not, such as doing big-stage magic when your expertise is close-up, you invite—guess what—heckling."

"Are you saying that you invited the drunken businessman to heckle you?" I asked.

"Bingo. Remember that I kept emphasizing how sharp the blades were? I was slowing the routine down—my guess is that it started to feel boring and annoying."

I nodded my head in agreement.

"By selecting someone who wasn't in the same condition as the rest of the spectators," Merlin said, "and by slowing the act down, I created a vacuum that needed to be filled. The drunken businessman filled it by trying to upstage me and undermine the act.

"Presenting new thinking is like presenting a magic trick. It requires an understanding of your audience and knowing how to act when they respond. In other words, selling innovation is performing! And just like performing you will find idea hecklers who will disrupt the 'performance' for a number of reasons:

1. **Territory.** It's not their idea and they feel threatened.
2. **Control.** The idea heckler negates your idea in order to assert his authority.
3. **Risk aversion.** The idea heckler has a limited ability to think differently out of a fear of failing or not feeling empowered to take the risk.
4. **Reality check.** The idea heckler may have a valid point; you have a bad idea.
5. **Poor preparation.** You haven't properly prepared the presentation or thought out the idea.

Merlin's comments made me think of Shawn and his resistance to so many of the ideas we discussed as a group. I had always thought he just lacked the ability to consider change. I reflected on some of the ideas he rejected and realized that perhaps they were not very well thought-out, that he was right to try to cut off discussion. I shared this with Merlin.

"Innovative solutions are not like the punch lines of jokes, where you either get it or you don't. New ideas have to be presented with the expectation that the audience will not understand. After all, thinking differently produces ideas or solutions that haven't been conceived before and therefore take time to digest. Besides, you must always deal with the 'Circle of Anxiety.'"

I looked at him with great curiosity and asked, "What is the Circle of Anxiety?"

He took out a napkin and outlined the process.

THE CIRCLE OF ANXIETY

You are asked to create something new.
New means something that has not existed before.
New ideas are unknown concepts.
The unknown creates anxiety.
No one likes to be anxious.
The easiest way to eliminate the anxiety is to avoid the unknown; in other words—kill the new ideas that were solicited in the first place.

"You are saying that great ideas are killed because of someone's anxiety!" I cried.

"That is exactly what I am saying, and the more you acknowledge that, the easier it is to avoid the wrath of the idea heckler."

"How?" I blurted out.

"By asking yourself these questions. Assume your ideas are great:

1. Is the presentation boring, thus inviting criticism?
2. Are you coming across as the 'only one who could have thought of this great idea,' thus losing connection with your potential supporters?
3. Have you taken the time to think them out and present them in a way that can be absorbed and understood by the group?

"One way to address these questions is to script what you are going to say and how you are going to say it," said Merlin.

"You mean doing a PowerPoint presentation?" I suggested

"No. PowerPoint presentations give their creator a false sense that everything is well thought-out," he exclaimed. "Everything feels orderly, but the ideas can still be jumbled! Imagine if I did a magic show using a PowerPoint presentation. That's not the answer."

Trying to show off my magic acumen I made the mistake of suggesting that he was referring to the term "patter."

Wrong again. "Patter is just talk," scolded Merlin. "A good company or service that is making a presentation or trying to sell doesn't use patter. They use a script that lets them control the situation. A great business script has a single point that lets the prospect walk away with a specific message or visual.

"Eugene Burger, voted one of the top one hundred magicians in the United States, taught me this," said Merlin. "Eugene looks like a handsome Santa Claus with a perfectly trimmed white beard that softly flows down over his chest. His performance is a work of art—he speaks slowly and seductively, often pausing between thoughts, allowing the audience to react to the impossible effect they just witnessed or reflect on what they are seeing. Everything Eugene does feels spontaneous. Nothing is. Eugene believes that every word counts. Nothing in his script is superfluous.

"A great script allows you to come across as relaxed and spontaneous," said Merlin. "In fact, I used Eugene's script when dealing with the drunken heckler onstage. Just as importantly, the script gives you the opportunity to handle the unexpected. The prop you are using may break down, the candle you are using just won't light, the vase you fill with water begins to leak, the participant you select from the audience and bring up onstage doesn't speak any English.

"A great script keeps you alive when your PowerPoint dies. Or when the CEO of the company unexpectedly shows up to a meeting," he pointed out.

"Unfortunately, we like to skip scripting," Merlin added. "We focus on the things we are most comfortable with, like putting down all our key thoughts in the PowerPoint presentation. Or making sure we have directions to the meeting or enough sandwiches if it's a lunch conference. We'll focus on pricing, making sure we cover our company's key benefits. We might type up an agenda and even do a rough rehearsal.

"And we might get away with it," he said. "But who wants to 'get away with it'—eventually it will not work. You want to get results every time you perform—selling a great idea should not be left to your charm or chance. So start by scripting your act—it's never fun or easy, and it takes time. But once it's done you can use it over and over, revise it, and improve it. The reality is that plotting out the performance saves you time and energy and provides the greatest chance of generating successful results."

"But who has time to script out every idea? It's just not practical," I argued.

"I guess the answer lies in the importance of the idea. New

ideas that will have little impact need less script attention. But if you are working on a new idea that has the potential to revolutionize your business, the more you script out the idea, the better.

"Here are some questions to consider: What is the first thing you are going to say when you present the ideas? What is the tone of the meeting: friendly, hostile, or indifferent? What approach will you take to address that tone? Why are you presenting the ideas in the first place? What are the potential flaws? How are you going to address the circle of anxiety the new ideas create? Who is going to be the most anxious? (Usually the person who has to approve or kill the idea.)

"The other benefit of scripting is that it often leads you to a new twist on the idea, a new way of presenting the idea, or even more amazing, a new and better idea," Merlin concluded.

I began to think of our new business ideas and some of the objections that Shawn and others raised. I made a note to talk to Chief about taking a stab at scripting some of his ideas and watching the group's reactions. I was about to ask Merlin to elaborate on the techniques for "selling great ideas." He must have given me a "cold reading" because he began to outline techniques to use.

CHECKLIST FOR LESSON #4

Idea Heckling—Removing the Obstacles to Thinking Differently

This lesson discussed in detail the reasons why great ideas get killed. Below are quick tips on how to increase the success of selling innovative thinking.

1. Be prepared. Make sure the ideas or solutions are well thought-out. Many people think great ideas should be naturally understood, like the punch line of a joke. But great ideas are not like jokes; they are like visions. And sometimes the person developing the idea has to work to help the other person see the value of the idea and the direction it is heading. A crucial way to ensure this is by creating a great script.

2. Create interaction. The best ideas are bought, not sold. Use the technique of preengagement to get your audience involved in the idea even before you present it. Set the stage by telling a story that involves and connects with your audience. Most magic tricks take only a minute to do, but a master magician can make them into a twenty-minute routine by getting everyone involved in a story where the punch line (the real magic) doesn't happen until the very end.

3. Be honest. It's common to fall in love with your first idea. Overcome the "love factor" by creating two more equally great ideas. Then explore each idea in depth. This provides you with a choice of solutions and alternatives and lets you avoid the mistake of working to sell yourself on a weak idea or an idea that needs more thought and development. People who don't do this figure that, if they keep repeating the idea to anyone who will listen, somehow the idea will improve and gain acceptance. Trying to convince someone of a bad idea is the fastest way to lose credibility.

4. Shut up and listen. Half the time, ideas are dismissed instantly because the person doing the dismissing perceives that their input was not being listened to or acknowledged. Don't cut anyone off. Let people bring up their reactions and their ideas. Take notes as they talk. Act interested even if you think they are off the wall. Consider their suggestions. Sometimes, to your surprise, they point out an obvious flaw that wasn't so obvious to you. Many times great ideas have come by listening to suggestions that at first seem plain dumb. But sometimes they seem that way only because you're having trouble understanding the other person's point of view. Try to see things through their eyes—new possibilities will occur.

"I love the story," laughed Merlin, "about the advertising guy who presented a storyboard—pictures and words—to a group of high-level executives. He was looking for them to sign off and allow him to go ahead and produce a commercial. The key decision maker refused to give the nod. The advertising guy's instinct was to keep talking, but instead he decided to listen. He asked the decision maker a simple question: 'What would you like to change in the commercial?' Turns out the decision maker thought the lead spokesperson in the commercial should be wearing a blue tie, not a red one.

"The advertising guy took out a marker, colored the tie blue, and showed it to the decision maker. The nod was given and the commercial produced. Over a half-billion dollars in sales was generated from the advertising."

The lesson here is *shut up* and *listen.*

---

5. Present multiple solutions. You increase the odds of getting approval or support by increasing the decision maker's scope of choice and control. This puts more pressure on you to come up with two or three more great ideas, but you need to do this anyway since there is never just one "great idea" or "business solution."

Merlin concluded the lesson by performing the French Drop, a sleight-of-hand trick allowing the magician to make a coin disappear and reappear elsewhere—in the other hand, inside a pants pocket, or even from the nose of a spectator.

Then I got the real surprise. Merlin began to show me how the French Drop was done, and for the next twenty minutes he took me through every move until I could do it myself.

"OK, you got the move down pretty well. So here's your homework for next week," he said with a twinkle in his eye.

Up to this point, I was having a lot of fun, but that quickly changed as Merlin explained the next assignment. I couldn't believe what he was telling me to do at our next session. Suddenly my nerves were shattered and I wondered how I would get through the next few weeks.

Fortunately, when I got back to the office, I had lots of issues that would soon preoccupy me. Buddy had secured a meeting with a new customer who had the potential to significantly increase our revenue. When Buddy gave me the good news he couldn't help but start with a story.

"I was at a local bar," Buddy began, "watching a football game with my friends. Halftime was boring, so I did that card trick you had taught us after one of your lessons with Merlin. Before I knew it, a group of people was standing around watching to see what card showed up on my cell phone. Everyone was blown away. They asked how I did it (very well, I said). One guy said he knew a couple of card tricks as well, and we began talking. I shared how I came to learn the trick and when I mentioned Merlin, he gave me a big smile. Turns out he is a member of the Society of American Magicians and knows Merlin, too. He is also our new prospect."

Buddy and I looked at each other with big grins on our faces. This was definitely great news and I was looking forward to sharing it with the team, as well as testing out some of what Merlin had just taught me about dealing with idea heckling.

In the next meeting, Buddy began by announcing the new prospect. Cheers and congratulations flew in his direction, and we then spent the next hour and twenty minutes discussing who needed to do what to help him pitch the business.

I decided we had enough that day and told everyone that I wanted a whole new round of ideas that we never dreamed possible.

"You have twenty-four hours," I said.

"You're killing us, Jonathan," said Chief.

"We've got a full plate," said Deborah. She pulled out her list to prove her point.

"Look, I want this to be fun. This is your time to daydream. There are no wrong or right answers. In fact, the silliest idea gets a prize. Besides, we are going to have the meeting at Joe's. My treat."

"Awesome," said Sunjay.

"Is this in the budget?" asked Thelma.

"Why Chinese?" Shawn asked.

Everyone else seemed happy with the idea of meeting outside the office. Besides, they love the food at Joe's. Though I wasn't sure if Shawn did.

Joe's real name is Joe's Shanghai. And in my opinion, it is one of the top ten Chinese restaurants in New York, which is quite something since there must be more than a thousand Chinese restaurants within a ten-mile radius. This restaurant has made soup dumplings famous. Originally only available in China, these are soft wontons stuffed with crabmeat or pork and filled with a wonderful-tasting soup that flows out and into your mouth. It's an explosion of flavor.

The next day, I arrived early to secure a large but private table near the back of the restaurant. I figured if things got ugly when I tried to apply Merlin's guidelines certain people would be predisposed not to make a scene.

Everyone arrived shortly after. I asked if it was OK if I ordered and everyone agreed. Even Shawn.

"I just want you to know I cannot have peanuts," Deborah announced.

"The prices seem reasonable," Thelma piped up.

I ordered. Then I literally opened the "table" for discussion to explore their new ideas. Deborah suggested that we could open a spa specializing in rejuvenating oils.

"I love the idea," said Buddy, "but it raises an important issue. We know about containers, oil, and food items. But shouldn't we be concerned about getting into the spa business — a business we know nothing about?"

Deborah responded quickly, and I anticipated a fight. Instead she surprised everyone.

"I love this idea, too," said Deborah, "partly because it's mine and I can visualize it. But Buddy is right. I propose we keep this idea on the list but focus on solutions closer to our comfort level of business."

The team agreed. So far, so good. Chief then suggested another idea.

"Why don't we offer traveling events?" he said.

Everyone waited for Chief to continue explaining, and he did.

"We fly to Europe quite frequently," Chief said.

"I know," said Thelma. "I'm the one who has to pay the travel bills."

Chief continued: "We do this to meet with various olive growers and manufacturers. We know the large vineyards and the smaller, more secretive places. Personally, business has taken me to really cool places that my friends, who travel the world, have never been to. In fact, I've sent friends to a small, private bed-and-breakfast in Spain owned by one of our clients. They loved it, and you know what the highlight of the trip was? They came back with olive oil made from the olives in the vineyard owned by the B&B. My friends had never tasted olive oil that was that freshly made. They've already booked a trip back for next year. There have to be lots of people like them who would love to do an olive oil tour and tasting."

I could see the group listening. Before responding we took a pause as the soup wontons appeared—along with a plate of sautéed snow peas to be placed on the giant turntable that allowed us to spin the food around to everybody. Next, a steaming colander arrived filled with clams cooked in beer. Everyone was enjoying their meal and feeling pretty good until Shawn spoke up.

"But what about our comfort level?" said Shawn. "I mean, are we going to become booking agents? Offer frequent-flyer points? Start negotiating with hotels? This is a waste of our time."

I had never seen the group get angry so fast. Shawn's attitude was ruining the spirit of fun. They were tired of Shawn's idea heckling and I saw Sunjay about to comment in a way that would lead to war. I interceded.

"Shawn," I said in a neutral tone. "You may be right. But let's say if we could manage all those things, how could you make the idea work?"

The table went silent.

Nobody ate.

Everyone stared at Shawn.

Shawn stared at me. Then he said, "You're kidding, right? Don't you want to know why I think the idea won't work?"

I looked Shawn directly in the eye and told him, "I would. But first I'd like you to try putting in the same energy you used to tell me why it won't work into telling me why it can work. Your ideas have merit and the group would like to hear them."

Shawn broke eye contact and was suddenly staring down at something between his stomach and the edge of the table. Then he looked up and spoke. "First off, I don't think it's that bad of an idea. It's just that some of the ideas I had suggested a few weeks ago were better."

Deborah, who was sitting next to me, was about to say something. I patted her arm in a way that told her to stay silent.

"But," continued Shawn, "to improve this idea I'd add an optional cooking or cheese- or wine-tasting experience. I mean, if these people are into olive oils they are going to be into the other things as well. In fact, one of our customers, Rob Kaufelt, who owns Murray's Cheese—a landmark gourmet shop in the West Village—was talking about offering a cheese-tasting event in Spain or Italy. Perhaps we could team up, share marketing costs, and pool resources."

Hearing ideas that reduced costs made Thelma shout out, "I second that suggestion!"

"We all know different people specializing in gourmet foods," Deborah joined in. "Let's sponsor a get-together, throw out our ideas, open the floor to discussion, then listen and learn. We might even get them excited and find a new partner or two to do this with."

This was better than watching Merlin levitate himself two feet above the stage. I felt like I had just witnessed a change in the group dynamic. By engaging Shawn, giving him the attention, and providing a platform for him to speak and for us to listen, I had allowed the process of idea generation to continue and grow.

I decided I would use this opportunity as a good example of dealing with idea heckling. I wouldn't use that exact term at this lunch because I didn't want to single out Shawn. Instead, I would discuss the principles. But first things first. The crispy duck had arrived.

MAGIC TRICK #4

Matching Wits

You can do this trick anywhere. It requires no sleight of hand. It also serves as a reminder that no matter how convinced you are of something, you may not always be right. But it serves another lesson: Never make your participant feel stupid. The script supplied makes you both the dunce and magician at the same time.

Effect: A participant counts out the number of matches in a matchbook. After confirming the number, take one of the matches out and light it. When the matchbook is opened again, the participant discovers that the original count is still the same and that one of the matches is burned.

Method: Before performing, bend down one of the matches in front of the matchbook, but do not remove it. Close the cover and light the match, then blow it out.

Now remove enough matches from the matchbook so that nine matches remain, plus the one you just burned (ten all together).

Close the cover, leaving the burned match bent down in front of the closed cover. When you are ready to perform, do the following:

1. Display the matchbook at your fingertips, with the burned match concealed beneath the thumb.

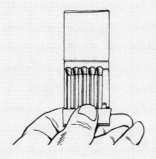

2. Open the matchbook cover.

3. Flick each match in the book to show how many are there. Ask the participant to count them off as you flick each one. As you flick each match, bend it slightly at the base. This will hide the bend in the burned match when it's revealed.

4. Pull out one match.

5. Bring the cover back over the matchbook by angling your wrist back, tilting the interior of the matchbook toward yourself. Remove your thumb from the burned match, then use the thumb to secretly flip it up into the matchbook as you close the cover.

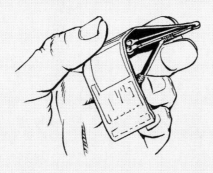

6. Light the match, then hand the closed matchbook to the participant. Blow out the match, and, in the act of reaching into your pocket to pull out the "imaginary magic wand," leave it there.

7. Rub the "magic wand" over the pocket, then over the matchbook, and have the participant open the matchbook.

8. They will find nine matches inside, but now one of them is burned.

For a more advanced illusion, you can vanish the match at step 6. Refer to Magic Trick #5, the French Drop, for an excellent method of vanishing the match. After you light the match and hand the matchbook to the participant, blow it out. Take it in the left hand and execute the French Drop, apparently taking it with the right hand, but secretly leaving it in the left. The left hand goes to the pocket to remove the imaginary magic wand (or a real one, for that matter), leaving the burned match there. Wave the wand over the hand, then over the matchbook. Finish as above.

Performance: "I once met a magician who told me I didn't have the wits to count. When he saw the look of anger on my face he offered to put it to the test. I accepted, and he pulled out a matchbook just like this." (Pull matchbook out of your pocket while covering burned match.)

"'Please count out the number of matches in this

matchbook,' said the magician." (Ask participant to count with you.) " 'Just to make sure, let's count again. OK, how many do I have?'

"I said to the magician, 'You have nine matches.' He agreed. He then said, 'I will take one out and light it. Please hold the matchbook while I get my magic wand.' " (Act like you can't find it at first, then mime pulling out a wand about twelve inches long.) "Ah, here it is." (Rub your imaginary magic wand first over your pocket, then over the matches.) " 'How many matches do I now have?'

"Of course I said, 'Eight.'

" 'This is where we match wits,' said the magician. 'I say we have nine. Please open the book and count again.' " (Give it to participant to open and count.) Finish by saying, "I'll never match wits with a magician again!"

DISCOVERING YOUR COMPETITIVE EDGE—"WHAT'S YOUR MAGIC?"

People at the office thought I had a stomach problem that week. I was running into the bathroom every twenty minutes. Merlin had made me promise to practice, practice, and practice the new trick he just taught me.

"Performing is one giant ongoing magic lesson," said Merlin. "It requires consistent practicing and constant feedback. You need to improve what works and eliminate what doesn't. The process for perfecting a magic show is the same for your business; it needs constant revisions, adjustments, and new ideas that bring you fame."

So here I was, locked in the bathroom. I wasn't liking Merlin at all at this moment. I practiced, for what felt like the millionth time, relaxing my fingers in a way that allowed me to keep the audience from guessing what I was doing while I directed their attention elsewhere. To aggravate matters, I was constantly revising my script in hopes of improving the performance. Yet as much as I disliked the task at this moment, I had to reluctantly agree with Merlin's advice because my act was starting to take shape in a way that I hadn't expected.

The day of my fifth lesson arrived and my anxiety took over. I left my office late. As a result I found myself running to my appointment, taking the stairs to the magic shop three at a time. By the time I reached the top of the stairs and walked into the shop, I was huffing and puffing. Merlin was also puffing. He was behind the counter, blowing up a clear balloon the size of a small beach ball. He tied a knot at the end of the balloon, pulled cotton out of his pants pocket, and stuffed the cotton in his ears.

"You never know when these suckers will burst," he said as he twisted the cotton tighter in his ear.

He then took a thin, very sharp twenty-four-inch-long needle threaded with a long red ribbon and pushed it completely through the giant balloon. Nothing happened.

"Here," yelled Merlin. "Take the needle and you try."

I grabbed the needle, and the moment it touched the balloon, it burst with a loud POP!

Merlin bent down to pick up the pieces.

"That was fantastic," I told him, "and I am sorry for being late." He didn't look up. "Sorry for being late," I repeated a little louder.

Merlin took the cotton out of his ears and looked up. "By the way, you're late," he said.

"Sorry," I said for the third time.

"It often happens to many of my students before this lesson," he said with a smile. "So relax. Today I am going to reveal to you one of my greatest secrets. And you will not learn it alone."

I was excited by the promise of learning something extra special, but also confused by his statement since there was no one else in the magic shop.

"Holly-polly, I can see that you've never been to the green room. You're in for a treat, kid." Merlin smiled. "Follow me."

He led me past the glass counters and down a hallway toward the bathroom. Just before reaching the bathroom we stopped. I was surprised that I hadn't seen the doorway I was now facing. It was a large oak door, and set into the panel was a beautiful square of stained glass designed with all kinds of magic icons including a rabbit, top hat, and floating lady.

"Go ahead and open it," said Merlin. But as I reached down, I discovered there was no doorknob. I tried pushing on the door and it wouldn't budge.

"Imagine you are in a movie, in a magic shop, and you have to get through a door that won't open because it has no doorknob. What's the first phrase you think of to open it?" he asked.

I actually thought of two phrases, "open sesame" and "abracadabra." Taking a guess, I went with the latter.

"Abracadabra?" I said foolishly. The door opened.

"Sometimes you have to give people what they expect," laughed Merlin.

I was too busy standing at the door probing for the secret lock to notice the other people sitting in the room. At first, they didn't see me either. Their attention was focused on the cards in their hands.

I counted four beautiful and ornate green-felt tables with three people per table. They were shuffling cards, dealing them, and then spreading the cards out in a perfect pattern, which in magic lingo is referred to as fanning.

"I'll teach you that one day," whispered Merlin. "The trick is to know where to place your fingers when you begin the move and to know how to use a special powder to make the cards fan evenly."

In front of the tables was a small stage with a black curtain backdrop and polished light wood floors.

"Jonathan, I'd like you to meet your fellow 'compeers,'" Merlin said with a sweep of the hand. "This is a term we use when we refer to our fellow brotherhood of magicians."

I was soon to discover that my "compeers" were from different types of businesses and had been taking lessons for the same reasons I had.

Introductions were made. I met Robert, head of corporate strategy at a world-famous global manufacturing company; Anthony, an executive from a big advertising agency; Kate, principal in a small financial advisor firm; Sheila, head of operations at a technology company in Europe; and Larry, the owner of a family bottle-supply business. In total, there were a dozen interesting businesspeople sitting in the room. They were all searching for new ways to think differently to energize their business and gain a competitive edge.

"Attention, everyone," called Merlin. "Your last assignment was to practice the French Drop and turn it into a routine. As you may have figured out, each one of you will be asked to perform today. I can tell by the clattering of coins in your pockets that we have a very nervous bunch of students. So to put you all out of your misery, and without further ado, let's start the show *now*! Jonathan, since you were the last here, why not go first?"

Up to that moment, I was feeling pretty confident about performing this trick. But the thought of going first in front of a group of strangers quickly diminished whatever confidence the hours of practicing had given me. I began to sweat, my stomach turned, and I wanted to run away. Why did I have to go first?

Everyone's eyes were on me. I had no choice but to step onto the stage. It felt as if I were about to walk a tightrope over Niagara Falls. I began to appreciate Merlin's insistence that I prepare a script.

"They say that time travel does not exist," I began. "But I disagree, and I will prove it. Is there someone with a quarter I can borrow?"

Austin, who owned a chain of dry-cleaning stores, raised his hand holding a quarter.

"Thank you, Austin. Please step up here along with your quarter and read the date on the coin and note any visible marks, so we can confirm its identity later," I said with a bit of a quiver in my voice. Austin concentrated on the quarter, noticing a tiny scuff on one side and a date: 2001.

I took Austin's coin in my left hand and swooped it into my right. My left hand was visibly empty.

"Austin, please grab my right hand and hold it tightly. And Kate, would you please come up and hold my empty hand?

"Time travel allows you to move back and forth through space without any restrictions. Walls, boxes, and cages cannot hold any object during time travel. While this gentleman is holding my hand and this lovely lady is holding the other, I'd like everyone to please count backward, starting at ten."

As the group counted backward, my body began to shake, my eyes rolled, and my arm began jerking up and down.

"I hate when that happens," I said with a smile. "Time travel does have its side effects. But it's worth it as we are now back in time. Now Austin, please let go of my right hand holding the coin and open it up."

The coin was gone.

"Kate, please let go of the empty hand, and open it up." She did and saw that the coin was inside. Austin examined the coin and confirmed it was his. That was everyone's cue to clap. I bowed to the audience and felt the trickle of sweat flow down my back.

"Supendo-mendo," said Merlin. "You could work on your technique a little, but you performed with a wonderful flare.

"Allow me to propose something to think about next time you perform the French Drop," he said kindly. "In the beginning, you asked Kate to hold your 'empty hand.' Never call attention to your hand in that way; someone may challenge you to open your hand. If they believe the coin is in the left hand and you ask them to hold your right, they will assume the right is empty. This is the power of inference; the participant will draw his or her own conclusion without your saying a word. Another example is when you want to demonstrate a hat is empty; instead of saying, 'There is nothing in the hat,' which may raise the suspicion that something actually is in the hat, just turn the hat upside down. If nothing falls out, the participant assumes the hat is empty even though it might be filled with a rabbit, a ten-foot silk, and an orange. Using the power of inference is a skill that comes with practice, confidence, and experience.

"But again, bravo for a great first performance," said Merlin.

I felt elated. I had praise from Merlin and the pressure to perform was removed. "Kate, since you are already onstage, why don't you perform next?" said Merlin.

Kate performed the trick flawlessly. I knew the method to the sleight of hand she was doing yet could not spot the hidden coin. Kate finished her routine in half the time I took, and with little scripting.

Larry, owner of the bottling supply company, went next and wasn't much of a magician. He knew it. On his first pass, the coin dropped out of Larry's hand. Picking it up, he sprained his back and then couldn't straighten it. Standing like a hunchback, he tried the pass again, except this time, he grabbed his tie, which dangled in front of his hand. Once he realized what he was holding, he let go of the tie and grabbed the coin with his right hand. Somehow he screwed up the sleight of hand so the coin was actually in the right hand and not in the left. So when he opened his right hand the coin fell out. He opened his left and found it empty and he was totally confused. His manner of performance was so funny, tears were running down our faces.

Over the next forty minutes everyone performed the same trick in his or her own style and manner. Afterward we all agreed how much fun it had been.

"I am proud of everyone," exclaimed Merlin. "Your reward for such a sterling performance is that I will reveal the greatest secret in all of magic!"

The room fell silent and he continued.

"The greatest secret in magic is this," Merlin said in a soft voice. "Great magic stems neither from the secret nor from the trick!"

We all looked at each other, reflecting a communal disappointment. After all, the secret is to magic what the recipe is to cooking; without knowing it, nothing can happen! Merlin must have sensed this but continued anyway.

"Our first reaction in witnessing magic is *awe*. Our second response, which happens in a deeper part of our psyche, is expressed in the question—how did he do that?

"In other words, deep down we want to know the secret of how to make 'the magic' happen—the secret that will turn our business around and make it grow 28 percent annually, the secret that will help us lose ten pounds and keep it off, and the secret that will make for a happier marriage.

"Yet look at what transpired in the last hour," said Merlin. "Everyone in the room knew exactly the same secret, yet performed the trick in completely different and compelling ways. This demonstrates an important lesson: The success or failure of how you performed did not depend on knowing the secret or the trick. It depended on how you approached *using* the secret—what script you chose and how you executed your performance.

"I call that difference knowing 'your magic.' Your magic is ingrained in your personality and makes up the essence of who you are. Your magic is that quality of you that makes what you do unique and totally special. In order to truly succeed, each of you must answer this question: What is *my* magic?" announced Merlin.

"Most members of my profession would agree that Houdini wasn't always a great magician," he continued. "His rapport with the audience when doing standard magic such as rope and card tricks put many to sleep. In fact, in the beginning Houdini billed himself as the 'King of Kards' and was almost forced to give up performing early in his career for lack of bookings.

"Luckily, an entertainment producer by the name of Martin Beck caught his act and marveled at his tricks with handcuffs. After the show he approached Houdini and made a deal: 'Give up magic, stick with handcuffs, and I'll make you famous.' The rest is history. Houdini went on to become the world's greatest death-defying escape artist.

"Houdini wasn't necessarily a nice person. He was highly egotistical and competitive, often stealing other magicians' secrets and tricks. Yet he was loved by the common man and admired by the wealthy and royalty. Magicians often debate the reason for Houdini's fame.

"One theory is that he was a European Jew who survived World War I, and his miraculous escapes represented his and every other European's escape from the wrath of the Kaiser. Others believe that Houdini's performances provided a sense of optimism, encouraging his audience to believe they could escape the shackles of poverty and despair. He was a small man struggling against the odds of the times, a struggle the masses faced every day.

"I believe Houdini's magic was providing hope!" said Merlin. "That was his true secret that went beyond the method or the trick. In our third lesson on creating a magical brand experience," he continued, "we talked about David Copperfield, and his magic is letting his audience discover him."

"What about Penn and Teller?" I asked. "They are one of my favorite magic acts."

"This dynamic duo's magic is truly unique." Merlin smiled. "They tell you when they are going to thumb their noses at you and then they even tell you how they are going to thumb their noses at you by explaining how the tricks are done. Their magic is making you feel foolish and smart at the same time in a way that makes you laugh and feel good.

"Let me repeat," said Merlin, "the secret of magic and of life is to answer this question: What's your magic? Everything else evolves from there.

"Think about it, ladies and germs," he exclaimed. "All of us in this room shared the secret move to do the French Drop. Yet knowing the secret did not make you a great prestidigitator. What will make you a great artist is knowing your magic.

"Jonathan, you are a great storyteller and actor. Kate, storytelling isn't your strength; technique is. And Larry, I can't tell if you really can perform the French Drop or not, but it doesn't matter. Your ability to embarrass yourself in front of the audience in a way that makes us laugh…that's your magic!

"Knowing your magic also gives you the courage to change. Houdini knew his magic was providing hope by doing death-defying escapes. His most famous trick, the milk-can escape, was being threatened through overexposure as other magicians began mimicking the act. He could have hung on, but instead he walked away from this trick at the height of its success and went on to invent an even greater escape act, the Chinese water torture illusion. That's where he suspended himself upside down, hands and feet chained, in a clear tank filled with water, which was then locked on top.

"Knowing your magic also keeps you focused. Michael Dell's magic is understanding how to eliminate the middleman. He began 'practicing' this when he was twelve and started selling stamps directly to people, bypassing the traditional dealers.

"Michael Dell in both good and bad times never forgot that Dell provided something the middleman could not—a great price and a quality, customized product. Ted Waitt, founder and visionary of Dell's competitor Gateway, offered a different magic, though a similar service. He helped introduce revolutionary new products, such as one of the first affordable, large, plasma TV screens. But he lost focus on Gateway as a direct-to-consumer company when he committed Gateway to owning retail stores and thereby took on a new source of overhead. That formula makes it difficult to keep prices down and quality up in a direct-to-consumer world. This is one of the reasons why Dell's company valuation has completely overshadowed Gateway's."

"Aren't you really talking about Rosser Reeves's concept, the USP—Unique Selling Proposition?" asked Anthony, the advertising executive. "My profession employs this concept to entice customers to consider our products and switch brands. There are lots of classical examples such as Head and Shoulders, getting rid of dandruff, and Oil of Olay, keeping younger-looking skin."

"Uncle Barrel-feffer," retorted Merlin. "That question always comes up. So let me give you the simple answer. No. The USP is a one-dimensional concept designed to explain why advertising campaigns worked in the 1940s. It is the tool of product positioning—trying to position the product or service in the mind of the consumer to be recalled at a later date. Identifying a USP is ideal for creating a difference in a world of products where differences no longer exist. But it's not relevant for building a lasting relationship in today's competitive environment.

"Identifying your magic is the glue that holds the relationship together. It is the building block that helps connect your business with your customer, your employee, your vendor, your bank—everyone who is involved in your life and business. It's what people feel, even if they cannot articulate it. It's what drives the employees to continue to thrive. It's what makes the customers come back, again and again.

"Answering the question 'what's your magic?' is done by identifying the essence that makes you unique—the special part of your psyche. One of the best examples is what Maxine Clark, the founder of Build-a-Bear, said when I asked her what her magic was.

> *I think my magic is that I've always been "small." I've always been really sensitive to being anonymous. I don't want to be invisible. And the way you can be not anonymous and not invisible is by making a difference for people.*

"Remember the girl who wrote to Maxine about opening a store in Canada?" asked Merlin.

He handed me a crumpled printout of an e-mail Maxine had sent him. I read the e-mail, which felt more like a letter written in crayon.

MY BUILD-A-BEAR DREAM

By Chelsey R.

It all started when I was eight years old. I discovered a store where best friends are made, called Build-a-Bear Workshop, in a *Discovery Girls* magazine I was reading.

I visited the Web site and found out that Build-a-Bear Workshop was created just eight years ago by a lady named

Maxine Clark. She had a dream to make a place just for kids to have fun at when they go shopping with their parents. Build-a-Bear Workshop sounded like a fun and magical place to me and I really wanted to go there someday.

My dad and I searched the Internet and found out that the closest Build-a-Bear store was in the Northshore Mall in Peabody, Massachusetts, which is very close to Boston. My dad is a Red Sox baseball fan so he began to dream about going to Boston to see the Red Sox play baseball, and I began to dream about going to Build-a-Bear Workshop!

Finally, last summer, it was time to go! I knew all about Build-a-Bear and I was ready! I wrote a letter to the Northshore Mall store to tell them when I would be coming and to save me the stuff I would need to build a Bunny Big Ears.

The BIG day was on July 30th and I got the surprise of my life! When I walked in they knew who I was and they had lots of stuff saved for me! My whole family was surprised at the way they treated us and we were all happy. They even hung up my letter in the staff room! I had a great time making my Bunny Big Ears. I went to all the stations and gave her a heart and everything.

But the best part was that Maxine Clark sent a message to her workers at the Northshore Mall to ask me if I would cut the ribbon at the grand opening for a new Build-a-Bear Workshop at the Mic Mac Mall! Build-a-Bear Workshop was coming to Nova Scotia, the first store in the Maritimes. I said "Yes!" to cutting the ribbon. I didn't even have to think about it!

When I got home from Boston there was a parcel for me

from Maxine with lots of surprises in it. She even had some things for my mom in there. I guess she was thanking me for saying I would cut the ribbon! She made me very happy!

On Friday, when there was no school, I went to the Mic Mac Mall where my dream kept happening. I got to go on a stage with Maxine Clark and she told everyone about my letters and my ideas for Build-a-Bear and she presented me with a very special pink poodle made especially for me because I love pink!

I cut the ribbon with Bearemy, the mascot, and we used huge scissors. Even the mayor of Halifax, Peter Kelly, was clapping for me! There were lots of children in the store helping to make bears for the I.W.K. [health center], and I made one too. These bears get donated for kids who are very sick. Build-a-Bear Workshop makes lots of people happy!

The funny part was that there was a crazy photographer there from the *Chronicle Herald* newspaper and he kept chasing me around taking pictures. A journalist asked me lots of questions so he could write a story in the newspaper. I felt like a movie star!

Maxine and her husband, who everybody calls Papa Bear, are very special people. They told me to keep dreaming, because dreams can come true. My next dream is to visit the biggest Build-a-Bear Workshop in the world in New York City! I will have to save a lot of money. Who knows, maybe someday I will work there!!

Love, Chelsey
Grade 6
Section 18

Maxine told Merlin:

Her writing was very eloquent, but when I met her, her mother told me Chelsey did not have a lot of self-esteem and this had helped to change that. The fact that she wrote a letter to the chief executive officer of the company and she got a response in like ten minutes, this is empowering to kids.

Sheila cut in: "So you're saying that every individual has their magic that can be separate from the magic of their company."

"Give that lady a cigar," said Merlin. "You need to answer both questions, what is your magic, and what is the magic of your company? We've already identified our individual magic in performing. If we traveled as a group around the country, then we'd have to identify the magic of our magic troupe.

"Maxine defined the magic of Build-a-Bear quite differently than herself," said Merlin.

I think the magic for a Build-a-Bear Workshop is that they see every customer as a guest be they 3 or 103; they are all treated equally. It is easy in today's retail world to make a difference for your guests—sometimes all it takes is a simple thank-you. We've become this place where people can come and have this positively awesome—we say pawsitively pawsome—family experience. It's creative but it's not judgmental—our guests can never really make a mistake. Each and every experience is totally customized. If you have a friend and they're into Harley motorcycles and you can make them a bear dressed in all the Harley gear, they're going to open it up and be wowed. They're going to know you took the time to make it for them and you put a wish in it.

We all listened to Merlin. Then he gave us a pad of paper and asked us to provide a list of answers to the question "What's your magic and the magic of your company?" This was not an easy task, and it took me ten minutes before I could begin the list. As usual, taking the first step was the hardest. Here's what I wrote:

WHAT'S MY MAGIC?

1. I am good at building relationships. My great-great-grandfather's motto was "what goes around comes around." I believe that treating people fairly is part of my magic.

2. If I didn't have this family business, I'd be doing something in advertising and marketing. I love ideas and have always admired a great ad. Enjoying creativity is part of my magic.

3. When I am excited about something, I find it transfers to others. I guess you could say my passion about things is infectious and motivates others. That's magical.

4. I might dream about a career in advertising, but I love food, and this career connects me with restaurants, gourmet food supplies, kitchenware companies, and great chefs. I have a "magic" knack for knowing what tastes good and why.

Merlin came over to where I was sitting and looked at my list. "Very oogle-doodle," he said. "I didn't know all of these things about you. Now that you have listed your magic, what are you going to do with it?"

"Good question," I said to him. "Here are some of my thoughts. I've been managing the business for quite some time. I'm thinking of stepping out in the front lines. I'd be a great pitchman for American Dressing because I can be passionate about the product and win people's trust. I'm going to lead some of the oil-tasting tours to Italy and Spain and start giving lectures on olive oil at events and parties. I think the business needs more of a personality, and I'm confident that I can provide a presence that will work and sell product."

Then I added, "I dismissed an idea that I had for creating a book about people in America, but now I've thought it over and I've decided to pursue it. I know a great portrait photographer and will combine personal portraits on one side and people's suggestions for dressings on the other side. Perhaps I will call it *American Dressings and Dreams*.

"It probably sounds corny," I told him. "But when I talk about it I feel energized and positive. And that makes me think of even more ideas."

"That's the power of knowing your magic," said Merlin. "You're all right, kid!"

He looked me right in the eye when he said it, and it felt wonderful. I wanted to reach out and give him a hug. He must have sensed this because he suddenly said, "Today's our last lesson."

He saw the surprise in my eyes and continued quickly.

"I don't mean permanent last lesson," he said gently. "But I've been booked for some overseas shows. Besides, I think you need to focus now on everything you learned and put your energies into working with your team and trying to work things out. The sooner you test the waters with your ideas, the faster you'll find out what works and what doesn't. Your lessons with me are the beginning of a process, not the end. We can resume when I get back."

For a few minutes I didn't speak. But Merlin was right. We'd been slowly moving forward on a bunch of strategies, but my team and I had not been moving as fast as we could have. I think we all just assumed Merlin would continue to show us the way. Now it was time to put everything we had learned to the test. I remembered my dad once telling me, "You miss a hundred percent of the time if you never take a shot."

"I understand," I said quietly.

"So as your last assignment," he began, "please answer the question 'What is the magic of your company?' I'll be back after I check in on some of the other students."

I began to make a list. At first I was finding I wanted to write down my magic, but that felt like that I was saying that the company was *me*. But I am not the company. That's when it hit me.

WHAT'S THE MAGIC
OF MY COMPANY?

1. Harmony. We are a group of unique individuals who manage to work hard but enjoy being with each other and supporting each other.

2. Quality and value. We are one level below the most expensive products in price but equal to them in quality. This allows us to keep our prices in line with most of the competition, but provide a better-tasting product.

3. Relationships. Perhaps great-great-grandpa's legacy set the overall tone for the company. Everyone who works

---

here understands that it takes time to build relationships and they are our most valuable assets. Even though
face-to-face meetings are becoming a thing of the past, I
see people going out of their way to use e-mail to maintain
contact with our customers—often sending e-mails just to
ask about their families or to see if someone's animal is out
of the veterinary hospital.

4. Honesty and guts. I think the team is honest with
themselves. I think they were receptive to the lessons from
Merlin because they listened to me acknowledge that the
business was going south and that we needed to do some
new things. They had the guts not to run but to band
together.

"So," said Merlin, as he looked over my shoulder at the new
list. "What is the magic of your company?"

I was startled that he was behind me just as I finished my
list. But then again, he was called Merlin for good reason. I
told him: "Our magic is honesty and fortitude. People who deal
with us enjoy the experience because they know what they are
going to get and that we are in it for the long haul. If a problem
arises, it will be dealt with fairly and honestly. That's the magic
of our business. It will be the same regardless of whether we
end up spending our time selling olive oil, giving tours, or offering a new type of salad dressing."

I then realized, I never used the term "importing business"
to describe the company. Just like Maxine Clark never said she
was in the "toy" business. How magical is that? I thought to
myself.

MAGIC TRICK #5

The French Drop

Effect: A coin is visibly grabbed by the right hand, leaving the left hand empty. Yet when the right hand is opened, the coin is gone.

Method:

The absence factor: The mind does the trick. The eye sees a coin being held between two fingers. When the other hand completes the pass over the coin the eye sees the two fingers of the other hand in the same position, but no longer holding the coin. The mind registers the absence and perceives that the coin is gone, supporting the assumption that the coin is now in the other hand.

Technique: Hold a quarter in your left hand (right hand if you are a lefty) between the forefinger and thumb. Hold the hand palm up in front of you, at about the level of your breastbone, with the flat surface of the coin facing the participants.

Step one: Practice dropping the coin onto the base of the fingers of the left (or right) hand without moving the thumb and forefinger. Practice in front of the mirror until you make the drop without the fingers visibly moving or the coin falling out of your hand. The challenge here is to not close your hand once the coin falls onto your fingers.

Step two: The right hand forms a "mirrored C" with the thumb as the bottom part of the "C." The other fingers form the crease of the "mirrored C" with the forefinger on the top.

Bring the right hand to the coin in a grabbing action, with the thumb going under the coin and the other fingers over it. Just as the fingers cover the coin, allow it to secretly drop onto the base of the left fingers.

Your right hand should now be closed into a fist. There should be no pause as you continue the action by moving the right hand in a diagonal pattern up and to the right. It should end with the right hand to the right of your face, with the fist at almost eye level. The key is to follow the supposed path of the coin with your eyes and your head.

This is one of the basic principles of misdirection. The audience will look where you look.

Step three: Pretend to hold the "coin" in the right hand for a beat. Then with your other hand, reach into your left pants pocket or into a purse and as you drop the coin in the pocket/purse, grab a pack of matches that have been placed there ahead of time. Pull out the matches and ask the participant to take out one match to be used as a magic wand.

Performance: "I believe that we carry magic around with us all the time [pause] and I see that you don't believe me. That's perfectly natural. If you don't mind, would you reach into your pocket [or purse] and see if you have a quarter. Thanks." (Place the quarter in your left hand, ready to do the French Drop.)

Look at the date on the coin and say: "1995 [or whatever date]. A very good year . . . for quarters." (As you say this, perform the French Drop and look at your right hand as if it holds the coin.)

"Now where did I put my magic wand?" (Reach into your left pocket, drop the coin, grab the matches.) "Would you mind pulling a match out of the pack and waving it over my right hand? Ahh, I see you have practiced this before. Now watch." (Slowly unfold your right hand, finger by finger until you show the hand is empty.) Take your bow as you say, "You see, you do carry magic around with you all the time. You just didn't know it!"

PROFITING FROM MY LESSONS WITH MERLIN

It had been a week since my last lesson with Merlin, and West and Company had swung into full gear with an energy and passion I hadn't expected. Even Shawn's attitude had changed. He was progressively evolving into a team player and, now, was enjoying the process of working together, sharing and supporting ideas. Little did I know that this metamorphosis would challenge our assumptions in a big way.

It was on a Tuesday after a team meeting that Shawn walked into my office.

"Jonathan, I've been thinking," he said reflectively. "I didn't raise this issue in this morning's meeting for fear everyone would think I was trying to sabotage things. But I think it's time we challenge a very important assumption."

I wanted to let Shawn know that his ideas were important and responded with two words.

"I'm listening," I said.

"This salad dressing idea. You know I wasn't a big supporter of this. But I am beginning to see its potential. When I mentioned the concept to my girlfriend, she immediately suggested an idea for Georgia peach dressing. This American dressing concept is catchy."

I smiled inside as he continued.

"Buddy's really hyped about the idea, and he's talking to all the major supermarkets, feeling them out, taking their pulse, plugging for sales statistics. I think it's a mistake!"

My anger and frustration quickly erupted like lava shooting out of a dormant volcano. Hadn't we just spent a week meeting and planning this entire campaign? Perhaps Merlin's approach to idea heckling hadn't worked? Perhaps people don't change? The expression on my face must have betrayed my present feelings to Shawn, so he quickly followed up.

"I like the idea," he said a little too loudly. "I like Buddy. I understand why he's doing what he's doing. But before West and Company goes too far, we need to decide what type of salad dressing manufacturer we want to be. We are modeling this idea after the big players in the industry. I'd like to challenge the group to act like who we are—a small, smart, and talented company that doesn't have to be bogged down by the same constraints that the major manufacturers face. Let's look at the other hand and start creating our own rules."

I looked at Shawn. He looked at me. Then he handed me a printout from the Oklahoma State University food technology fact sheet.

It read:

> As U.S. consumers' tastes have grown more sophisticated over the years, salad dressing buyers have shown more interest in premium/gourmet sauces, condiments, and dressings. A wide variety of offerings have made their way into the market place: low-fat, low-carb, zesty new flavors, traditional flavors marketed in new ways, etc. The high level of household penetration and the varying ethnic and diet-driven demands

of consumers suggest that niche salad dressings can find means of competing with national brands.[1]

"When I read this," said Shawn excitedly, "I thought about what Peter van Stolk said. His advice was to first learn what the big companies do—then go ahead and do your own thing. His ideas gave me the confidence that there's lots of room to be different, and to be rewarded for it. This report supports that!"

A million thoughts whizzed through my mind, all at the same time. I thought of Merlin and the value of his lessons. I thought about Shawn and how people's ideas can be shaped by the way you react to them. I thought about the truth of what he was saying. But I said none of this. Instead I got up, walked over to Shawn, and gave him a half-hug/handshake.

"I think the group needs to hear this," I said to Shawn, "and I want you to be the one to tell them."

I could read the fear in his eyes—the fear of challenging the group—so I continued.

"If you have a few minutes we can work on your approach."

After a half an hour of further discussion I asked Shawn to script what he was going to say and e-mail it to me so we'd fine-tune it.

Two days later, Shawn challenged the team in a very inventive way. He took a bottle of Wish-Bone dressing in his hand, held it up, and said to the group, "Is this who we want to be?"

"I wouldn't mind their profits," said Thelma. Everyone, even Shawn, laughed.

"I think we've been looking at this hand too much," said Shawn, holding up his left hand. "I propose we look at the other hand and see where it takes us. I don't mean bag the

---

[1]E. Early, R. B. Holcomb, C. Willoughby, J. Brooks, and C. Stone. 2005. "A Market Evaluation of Salad Dressings." Oklahoma Cooperative Extension Service Fact Sheet FAPC-138.

idea. I mean let's give ourselves permission to really make our own magic."

"It'd be a lot easier to sell if we were a brand name," said Buddy. "But I have to admit, it wouldn't be very challenging. I think the reason the supermarkets are talking to me now is because we've got such an interesting idea. They want to know where it's going to lead."

"I look at the bottle and see, been there, done that," said Deborah. "I like the fact that we are different. It makes it more fun. Fun has energy."

I was proud of this team. They didn't go after Shawn or try to put him down. Instead I could see the ideas beginning to churn inside their minds. I reflected on Merlin's real magic—teaching us to become our own "magicians."

The next six weeks were spent laying out new ideas and thinking differently about our business.

It was then that I received a postcard from Merlin.

"Hey, kid, I'm teaching some international big brands new thinking. I can't name names or they'll kill me. Here's the e-mail address I never gave you. Send full report. Merlin. P.S. When you think differently, magic happens. (Even in six weeks.)"

Did he know what was going on at West and Company? Maybe this was his ultimate mind-reading act? Perhaps he had been in touch with Buddy? Rather than take the time to figure this out, I decided I'd write to Merlin.

To: Merlin@foolaboolamagic.com
From: Jonathan@westandcompanyolives.com
Subject: Re: The kid

Dear Merlin:

If you find this e-mail a bit long, it's your fault. You ignited a fire of ideas that no one wants to put out. Here's an updated list of what we've been up to since our last lesson. I'll tackle our work on American dressing first. If I have the energy, I'll fill you in on our olive-oil-on-demand business.

1. American dressing: We took the URL "americandressing.us" and are turning it into a community of like-minded people who enjoy food as well as having choice, control, and freedom over the quality of food they eat, especially salads, dips, sandwiches, appetizers, etc. Legally we will use the name American Homeland Dressing on our packaging. (American Dressing is too generic.)

2. Our line of dressings is growing beyond the original brand of American Homeland Dressing, which is made up of chunks of Wisconsin cheese, juicy New Jersey tomatoes, and smokey bits of Virginia bacon. New recipes include California avocado, Boston baked bean, Florida citrus, Seattle salmon, Kansas City barbeque, Chicago pizza, Alaskan king crab, New Orleans spiced Creole, Idaho potato, and Texas chile. We are also considering a line of condiments: New Jersey tomato ketchup, California relish, and New Mexico mustard.

This is just our list. On americandressing.us, we invite people to send in their own recipes. Winners will get their pictures featured on the bottle or a trip to their favorite place in America.

3. Speaking of bottles, Thelma and Shawn have been working with the bottle manufacturers on the price and logistics of creating bottle shapes on demand. They've created half a dozen interesting shapes, including the state of Florida, the Seattle Space

Needle, and Mount Rushmore. Sunjay is setting set up a section on the Web site that will allow people to suggest other bottle shapes as well.

4. We want the American Dressing line to provide interesting information to our customers about their cities or states or things relating to those locations. For example, our Seattle salmon dressing label is going to talk about the need to protect salmon from Washington State and what consumers can do about it. Our California avocado dressing will explain how avocados are picked and harvested—plus list where in California you can take tours of avocado farms. We want people to rediscover things they didn't know about our country.

5. Organic vegetables and foods are growing in demand, so we are exploring a line of organic American dressings that will also tie in and support all the local organic farms around the country.

6. Buddy and Chief are brainstorming alternate places of distribution. They're considering health clubs, spas, sports events like NASCAR races (Daytona orange citrus) and rodeos, local farm stands, museum stores that sell American artifacts, street souvenir stands in Washington, D.C. These are wild ideas, but Buddy is already getting interest from cooking schools and tourist stores in New York City.

7. We also decided to follow the other hand to look for ways to win the trust of our customers. Salad dressing can be low-fat or high-fat, and it's not easy to tell. No manufacturer in their right mind calls attention to the number of calories. We are! Each bottle is going to have a "Freedom Meter" that indicates the calories and fat in the dressing. At one end of the spectrum will be "Not So Free"; at the other end will be "Fat Free."

8. We discussed proposing a "buy American" day around July 4th weekend and have set up meetings with Detroit car manufacturers, American tool makers, and retail clothing stores.

9. Buddy's talking to Jones Soda about licensing their process for personalizing labels on the dressing. We are toying with the tag line: A Salad Dressing You Can Call Your Own, and we want people to have ownership of the labels.

10. We are quickly learning that salad dressing is not just for salads anymore. The list of potential extended uses for salad dressing is enormous: dips, sandwich spreads, casserole ingredients, even yogurts. So we are going to challenge our customers to explore the most interesting ways of using the dressing. We may use our labels to demonstrate usage or put the suggestions under the bottle cap.

11. Who ever heard of giving a salad dressing as a gift? It will happen with our dressing. Shawn is working on a strategy for releasing the dressing on a limited basis in certain states. Our goal is to create a word-of-mouth campaign that makes the indigenous dressing recipes exclusive, so they will have value to those who normally cannot get them—people like out-of-town tourists or visitors. For example, Louisiana Cajun dressing will be sold only in Louisiana and neighboring states, but you can have it shipped in a gift box to your aunt in Chicago.

12. Thelma suggested salad dressings that are fun for kids to eat. We are looking into a line of American dressing featuring famous American sport stars, presidents, or extreme, kid-friendly athletes like the Olympic snowboarder Shaun White. Buddy's talking

to Coke and Pepsi about dressing ideas that tie into their soft drink line. Pepsi-Cola owns Fritos, and we are thinking of a crunchy salad dressing that includes the Fritos chips. Sounds awful to me, but Max, my twelve-year-old, was pretty excited about the idea and even offered to help create the recipe.

13. Sunjay came up with the idea of turning the bottle caps into interactive devices. After you finish the dressing, we invite you to draw a smile or picture on the bottom of the cap indicating how much you enjoyed the flavor experience. Every month we'll show all the drawings on the Web site, select the best one for that month, and the winner gets a free case of dressing shipped to them.

14. I sent a proposal to a bunch of book publishers regarding the concept for *American Dressings and Dreams*. It contains portrait photographs that demonstrate people's love and passion for growing their own food, the lore of the American farmer, and Americans who create unique meals using American-based products. Their recipes will be featured in the book along with some imaginative American dressings. Three publishers have expressed interest in the project.

Well, I can keep typing, but my computer is getting tired, so I will sign off here. I'll update you on our olive-oil-on-demand business in the next e-mail. Hope your meetings went well. Look forward to hearing where you'll turn up next.

Best,
Jonathan

I pressed "Send." The next morning when I got to the office there was a reply from Merlin. It was short and to the point.

To: Jonathan@westandcompanyolives.com
From: Merlin@foolaboolamagic.com
Subject: Re: Re: The kid

Holla bolla! You're going to be more famous than Houdini.

I shared the e-mail with the team, and once again I saw that Merlin was able to apply his magic, this time from afar, by pulling smiles from their exhausted faces. The team was learning that the success of great ideas lies in the details and the execution. They were not only working on American dressing, but also on the olive oil on demand business. I quickly summarized this in my next e-mail to Merlin.

To: Merlin@foolaboolamagic.com
From:Jonathan@westandcompanyolives.com
Subject: Re: Re: Re: The kid

Dear Merlin,
    Here's what's happening with our other new act—olive oil on demand. This concept is just beginning to take shape in the United States, and I believe we can make it into more of a recognized business.
    The wonderful thing about food is that there is always a great story to tell. Olive oils, unlike wines, do not age well with time. In fact, most olive oils are past their prime in two years. Manufacturers have been known

to dilute their olive oils with other ingredients and are constantly being monitored. Some have even been sued. Yet the public isn't aware of this.

We are going to educate people about this. All of our labels will have dates indicating when the oil was harvested and bottled. On our Web site, we will sell oils based on their dates. The older they are, the less expensive they become. (Think Sy Syms, the man who founded a discount clothing store that marked down prices the longer the clothes stayed on the rack.)

An experiment to provide choice and control is taking place at the very moment I write this. We've constructed a Web site that provides visitors with the control to create their own package using a number of choices that no one else has offered.

Choose:

The country: Spain, Italy, France, Turkey
The date of the pressing: 24 hours, 30 days,
    6 months, 1 year
Flavor: Nutmeg, almond, peach
Bottle: Clear, dark green, long neck, short neck,
    cork, or screw cap
Size: 30ml, 250ml, 500ml, 750ml
Label: Standard label or you can send in a picture

If you recall, I mentioned that we own the building we are in. This has taught us about having real estate as part of our portfolio. My brother—who is a silent partner of the business—has a degree in agriculture and teaches as a career. He has agreed to investigate setting up olive groves in the United States.

Our strategy is twofold: purchase our own olive groves to test our ideas and provide fresh-pressed olive oil within forty-eight hours (no one offers this type of national distribution), and offer tours (like wineries).

Olive groves are not like vineyards. Grapes produce ten times as much profit per acre as olives do. We need to find cheap land in subtropical conditions, and we're concentrating our search in Florida, Texas, Arizona, and California (where there are a hundred small groves already). We believe the value of the land will escalate over time. If the olive oil business doesn't pan out, we will sell the property for a profit.

The United States produces less than 1 percent of the olive oil American consumers buy. Most domestic vineyards don't make money because they are in competition against imports from foreign vineyards that are subsidized by their native countries. This is forcing the domestic industry to challenge their assumptions and is stimulating new value-added opportunities.

West and Company is in a great position because we will be using both domestic and imported oils. Here is a list of some of those opportunities:

1. Olive oil on demand. Online and retail stores will deliver fresh-pressed olive oil within forty-eight hours.
2. Interactive labels. After you buy the olive oil you pull off a strip on the label that, once exposed to air, begins to change colors. When it turns red it means the oil needs to be replaced.
3. "Take Your Pick." We are developing a line of toothpicks with flags that have our olive oil logo on

it. The flags have the names of different olives and cheeses. You stick the flag in when you are serving appetizers to let people know what they are getting. These will be distributed anywhere that olives and cheese are custom-packaged.

I have some other good news. If you're heading to Italy perhaps we could hook up. I've been in correspondence with a number of the local olive vineyards, and they were very interested in hosting visitors and providing tours. Other tour companies are doing this but not providing the same kind of intimate experiences that we can provide because of our relationships that go back a hundred years. Our olive oil on demand business provides a pipeline of prospects as well.

By the way, my team voted me the "Lee Iacocca" of American dressing. They agree that my "magic" is my contagious enthusiasm. I'll become the company spokesperson. I will meet with the top chefs as well as with mayors from five major cities to get them to vote on the American Homeland Dressing flavors our customers select for their locations.

Finally, I have decided to follow the other hand about owning a family business. Times are changing too quickly, and good people are getting harder and harder to find. I've decided to challenge great-great-grandpa's assumption about keeping it in the family. I have been talking to my lawyer and doing the legal paperwork to restructure the company with the goal of making all the employees owners of the company. My brother and sister, who both own shares, agree.

You said to me that when you think differently, magic

happens. Now I understand. Thanks for all your help. To be continued . . .

Best,
Jonathan

It was the end of a long day and I shut down my computer. There was one more chore to do before leaving the office. I rummaged through my top desk drawer in search of something special that was given to me before I met Merlin for the first time. This item had taken on a new significance, and I was anxious to see its closure. Under my Michelin map of Italy, I found it—the check made out to Merlin and signed by Wilcox.

I recalled what Wilcox had told me when he recommended Merlin.

"I believe in George so much I will send you a check…If at any time you feel you haven't gotten your money's worth from one of the lessons, use the check."

Clipped to the check was Wilcox's business card. I took an envelope, wrote out his address, and popped in the check with a note.

"No thanks," I wrote. I knew Wilcox needed no further explanation.

To learn more about Merlin, his other lessons, and how he got to be so smart in business, visit http://followtheotherhand.com.

MY FAVORITE MAGIC TEACHERS, PLACES TO SHOP, AND MAGIC BOOKS

I could fill a book with all the great magicians who also teach; they are all extremely talented and are most giving with their time. The best way to meet them is by attending one of their lectures or shows. There are three major magic societies: Society of American Magicians (SAM), International Brotherhood of Magicians (IBM), and the Magic Circle (in the UK). I recommend logging onto their Web sites to find out when lectures and performances will be given at the local chapters of these groups. They are often open to the public.

Another source of "everything you want to know about magic" is the major magic magazines, *Genii* (geniimagazine.com) and *MAGIC* (magicmagazine.com). These are well written and highly informative about magic tricks, magicians, magic DVDs, and more.

MAGIC CLASSES

Jeff McBride's Magic and Mystery School (Las Vegas): It will change the way you think about magic and performing. Great for the layman who wants to understand how to stand and perform in front of a crowd, the semiprofessional looking to improve his or her act, or the magic hobbyist who wants to learn what real magic is all about.
Contact: jeff@mcbridemagic.com.

Cardone (NYC): Individual lessons for both children and adults. Contact:cardonethemagician@yahoo.com.

Eugene Burger (Chicago): If Eugene agrees to teach you, it's an honor and a treat. Close-up magic only as well as magic theory. He also teaches with Jeff McBride in the master class.
Contact: magicbeard@aol.com.

The Amazing Marco (Long Island, NY): With the patience of a saint and always with a smile, Marco teaches sophisticated close-up magic that requires plenty of practice, but it's worth it. He'll teach you the simple stuff as well.
Contact: beach9@optonline.net.

David Roth (NYC): He is one of the greatest contemporary sleight-of-hand artists and coin manipulators. It will be difficult to get a private lesson so I suggest purchasing his DVD lectures on coin magic—especially his lesson on coin retentions.

Magic Castle (Los Angeles): Magic lessons are offered at this mysterious private club outside Los Angeles, CA. But the real attraction is meeting and watching

world-famous magicians perform in a wonderful
Victorian atmosphere. Reservations are required along
with jacket and tie for men, and you must be the
guest of a magician, a member of a magic society,
or a member of the club. You can dine at one of
five dining rooms, followed by a theater show in the
Palace of Mystery. Contact: magiccastle.com.

MAGIC SHOPS

You can buy the magic tricks mentioned in this book at
these shops. Not all items are always in stock. These shops are
friendly and will provide answers. Just don't ask them to reveal
the secrets of the tricks before you make your purchase.

Magic, Inc. (Chicago): Founded by the Dean of Magic,
the late Jay Marshall. Tricks for children, hobbyists,
and professionals. One of the largest collection of
magic tricks available by catalog. If they can't find it
for you, it may not exist. Contact: Magicinc.net.

Tannen's (NYC): Founded by Lou and Irv Tannen
in 1925. It was the mecca of magic and is the
oldest magic shop on the East Coast. David
Copperfield, David Blaine, Criss Angel, and other
young magicians could be found here on a Saturday
afternoon watching (and learning) from some of the
greatest magicians. Those glory days of magic are
past, but Tannen's is still a destination to shop,
talk trade, hear lectures, and on special occasions
see a famous name magician in action.
Contact: Tannens.com.

Fantasma Magic (NYC) is both a line of prepackaged magic tricks distributed globally as well as a new magic shop near Madison Square Garden in New York City. The store integrates racks of Fantasma Magic products with beautiful glass displays of professional and custom, one-of-a-kind magic tricks. There is also a mini-museum with original Houdini handcuffs and other rare collector's items. Contact: Fantasmamagic.com.

Owen Magic Supreme (Azusa, CA): The Mercedes-Benz of magic shops. The catalog alone costs $32 (plus shipping) and is worth every penny. Order item number 4012 and you'll be shipped the equipment to saw someone in half. Call for item number 2307 and you'll soon be floating your assistant in the air. Pick out item number 803 and you'll own the 3" die box. Every trick is handmade with quality and confidence. Contact: Owenmagic.com.

Viking Magic and the Collector's Workshop (McAllen, TX): Quality tricks for the collector or perfectionist. These items include the original Gumball Machine, where a borrowed ring appears inside a plastic bubble randomly selected from the machine. You can order a video catalog of their most popular tricks being performed for $16.50. Contact: Vikingmagiccompany.com.

Abbott's Magic (Colon, MI): It's like visiting Merlin's shop. Great tricks of all kinds. The catalog illustrations of the tricks look old-fashioned, but these tricks are some of the best illusions available today. If you're looking to hold a bit of history in your hand while seeing the world of magic at a glance, pay $15 for their 500-page, 3-lb. catalog.

Contact: Abbottmagic.com.

Stevens Magic Emporium (Wichita, KS): A fun place
to shop online for magic tricks. Don't forget to check
out their extensive videos of magic tricks in action
that you then can purchase.
Contact: Stevensmagic.com.

MAGIC BOOKS

I have more magic books in my collection than I can pos-
sibly list. Here are a few of classics. Some may be hard to get.

Brown, Gary R. *The Coney Island Fakir: The Magical Life
of Al Flosso.* Tahoma, CA: L&L Publishing, 1997.

Christopher, Milbourne. *The Illustrated History of Magic.*
New York, NY: Thomas Y. Crowell Company, 1973.
(Also in an updated paperback version, published by
Carroll & Graf in 2005.)

Corinda. *13 Steps to Mentalism.* New York, NY: Louis
Tannen, 1968.

Dunninger, Joseph. *Dunninger's Complete Encyclopedia
of Magic.* New York, NY: Lyle Stuart, 1963.

Etcheverry, Jesús. *The Magic of Ascanio: The Structural
Conception of Magic.* Madrid, Spain: Páginas, 2005.

Fitzkee, Dariel. *Magic by Misdirection.* Pomeroy, OH:
Lee Jacobs Productions, 1975.

Houdini, Harry. *A Magician Among the Spirits.* 1924.
Reprint, New York, NY: Arno Press, 1987.

Reynolds, Charles and Regina. *100 Years of Magic Posters.*
New York, NY: Putnam Publishing Group, 1976.

Scarne, John. *Scarne on Card Tricks.* 1964. Reprint,
Mineola, NY: Dover Publications, 2003.

Slydini, Tony. *The Magical World of Slydini*. New York, NY: Louis Tannen, 1979.

Steinmeyer, Jim. *Hiding the Elephant: How Magicians Invented the Impossible and Learned to Disappear*. New York, NY: Carroll & Graf Publishers, 2003.

Tarbell, Harlan. *The Tarbell Course in Magic*. 1942. Reprint, Cranbury, NJ: D. Robbins & Co., Inc., 1971.

Vernon, Dai. *Dai Vernon's Select Secrets*. Philadelphia, PA: Max Holden, 1949.

ACKNOWLEDGMENTS

I couldn't have written this book without..." is found in the acknowledgments sections of almost all books. Now I understand why. It's true. My Board of Magicians, a group of successful businesspeople with a passion for magic, volunteered their valuable time to review every page of the manuscript. They fueled my confidence with enthusiastic praise balanced by an incredible attention to the detail of the writing — correcting misplaced facts, challenging my thinking, and even editing the text. These unique individuals are Marc DeSouza, Ralph Guild, Larry Reichlin, Nick Pudar, Gary Mandelblatt, Marc Eisenoff, and Cardone.

Every idea has a birth date, and I want to thank my business peers and friends who were there at its birth and helped nurture its growth: Stan Rapp, Mark Hughes, Jeremy Koch, Jim Walter, John Ovrutsky, Bob Katz, Marc Glickstein, Don Heyman, and my brothers, Rich and Doug Cohen.

My Great-uncle George taught me magic, but the person who taught me the magic of writing a proposal, marketing a book, and nuturing an idea is my literary agent, Esmond

Harmsworth. A thank-you goes to Stuart Brotman, who introduced me to my editor, Phil Revzin. If I ever get caught in a storm at sea, I want Phil as my captain. He has a talent for smooth sailing through the crests and waves of writing a book.

My wife, Deborah, took on multiple roles as she contributed to editing the manuscript, providing ideas for the book jacket, and codesigning the magic cards. Her love and support, and that of our son, Max, were invaluable. I am a lucky guy to have them in my life. Though creativity can be taught, it can also be inherited, and I have my mom and her genes to thank for always keeping me thinking and inventing.

Finally, I'd like to thank my Great-uncle George, Lou and Irv Tannen, Slydini, Al Flosso, Ed Michelle, Dunninger, Jeff McBride, Eugene Burger, the Society of American Magicians, and the world of magicians for letting me share part of their lives.

ABOUT THE AUTHOR

Andy Cohen helps people think differently and lead differently. His creative communications and learning firm works with global clients including Bosch, American Express, HSBC, Novartis and Nestlé. He's also an expert magician and served on the board of the Society of American Magicians, Parent Assemply #1. He resides in New York City with his wife, Deborah, son, Max, and cat, Boris.